WOMEN IN THE POETRY OF T. S. ELIOT

Women in the Poetry of T. S. Eliot

A Psychoanalytic Approach

Tony Pinkney

Excerpts from *Collected Poems 1909-1962, Four Quartets, Selected Essays, Murder in the Cathedral* and *The Family Reunion*, all by T. S. Eliot, are reprinted by permission of Harcourt Brace Jovanovich, Inc.; copyright 1932, 1935, 1936, 1950 by Harcourt Brace Jovanovich, Inc.; copyright 1939, 1943, 1960, © 1963, 1964 by T. S. Eliot; copyright 1967, 1971, 1978 by Esme Valerie Eliot.

First published 1984 by
THE MACMILLAN PRESS LTD
London and Basingstoke
Companies and representatives
throughout the world

ISBN 0 333 34706 4

Typeset by
Wessex Typesetters Ltd
Frome, Somerset
Printed in Hong Kong

*In memory of our dear son
Raymond Minow Pinkney*

Contents

Preface

Early in *Murder in the Cathedral* we hear that 'Several girls have disappeared / Unaccountably'. But this tantalising hint, promising a narrative at least as interesting as that more resplendent 'disappearance' which is Beckett's martyrdom, is never quite developed. Two vivid lines later in the text seem to belong to it:

> We have seen the young man mutilated,
> The torn girl trembling by the mill-stream.

And there is a final obscure allusion to 'the push into the canal'. 'We are not ignorant women', declare the Women of Canterbury, whose speeches these are; and they do indeed seem to know more than they are willing to tell. As we attend to their long choruses, we may well come to feel, for a brief, vertiginous moment, that the play's 'official' religious narrative is perhaps only a Formalist 'motivation of the device' for their catalogues of deprivation and daily pain or for those more lurid visions of 'the savour of putrid flesh' which terrorise them. It seems as if the energies of the text lie not so much in Beckett as 'In the guts of the women of Canterbury'.[1]

Such a foregrounding of the role and tribulations of women in Eliot's work will be the aim of this study, which will also invoke the psychoanalysis of Melanie Klein and D. W. Winnicott in an attempt to render those disappearances a little less 'unaccountable'. Delving behind the Oedipus complex into the most primitive phases of relationship between infant and mother, Klein and Winnicott focus critical attention on the commanding importance of representations of the mother and the female body in Eliot's texts. These two analysts have not, as far as I know, been systematically used in literary criticism before, yet both have powerful claims on the attention of feminist criticism.

Though my account of Eliot's verse is loosely chronological, I do not have a psychoanalytical narrative to tell. 'Hysteria' opens and

'Gerontion' closes my dealings with the poetry, in defiance of chronology, and my discussions are grouped thematically, as my chapter headings suggest. It has seemed more fruitful to use psychoanalysis to 'open up' the texts, to focus on the apparently marginal and to defamiliarise the well known, than to submit both poetry and drama to a teleology handed down by theory in advance. I have throughout aimed to be suggestive rather than exhaustive, and my own critical preference is decidedly for the intricate dialectic of the 'schizoid' rather than the more suave schematisations of the 'depressive position', for reasons I discuss at length below.

This book derives ultimately from Moira Megaw's decision many years ago to lock my copies of Leavis away; I am grateful to her both for that and for her teaching. I owe a long intellectual debt to Robin Jarvis and also to my old *Thumbscrew* associate Julian Pattison, whose incisive comments have cleared away much literary-critical lumber for me. Thanks too to Graham Whybrow, fellow Winnicottian, whose suggestion that Othello's handkerchief is a 'transitional object' has yet to be explored. I am deeply grateful to Terry Eagleton for his practical help and stimulating teaching during the writing of this work; to him I owe both the chance recommendations that directed me to Klein and Winnicott and the sustained encouragement that led me to persevere with them. To my wife, Makiko Minow, I owe the support, patience and continuing intellectual exchange which alone allowed me to complete this book. We dedicate it to the memory of our son Raymond, whose arrival made infant–mother psychoanalysis so exciting to me and whose death leaves it now so bitter and painful.

T.P.

Acknowledgements

The author and publishers wish to thank the following who have kindly given permission for the use of copyright material:

Faber & Faber Ltd, and Farrar, Straus & Giroux Inc., for the extracts from T. S. Eliot's *On Poetry and Poets*, *To Criticize the Critic*, *Knowledge and Experience*, *Elder Statesman* and *Poems Written in Early Youth*.

Faber & Faber Ltd, and Harcourt Brace Jovanovich Inc., for the extracts from T. S. Eliot's *Selected Essays*, *Murder in the Cathedral*, *Confidential Clerk*, *The Family Reunion* and *Collected Poems 1909-1962*.

Faber & Faber Ltd, and Harvard University Press, for the extracts from T. S. Eliot's *The Use of Poetry and the Use of Criticism*.

List of Abbreviations

CC T. S. Eliot, *To Criticize the Critic*, 2nd edn (London: Faber, 1978).

CP T. S. Eliot, *Collected Poems 1909-1962* (London: Faber, 1963).

EEY Lyndall Gordon, *Eliot's Early Years* (London: Oxford University Press, 1977).

FR T. S. Eliot, *The Family Reunion* (London: Faber, 1963).

FS T. E. Hulme, *Further Speculations*, ed. Sam Hynes (Minneapolis: University of Minnesota Press, 1955).

IF *The Image in Form: Selected Writings of Adrian Stokes*, ed. Richard Wollheim (Harmondsworth: Penguin, 1972).

IP *Imagist Poetry*, ed. Peter Jones (Harmondsworth: Penguin, 1972).

JL Anika Lemaire, *Jacques Lacan*, trs. David Macey (London: Routledge, 1977).

OPP T. S. Eliot, *On Poetry and Poets* (London: Faber, 1957).

PEY T. S. Eliot, *Poems Written in Early Youth* (London: Faber, 1967).

PR D. W. Winnicott, *Playing and Reality* (Harmondsworth: Penguin, 1974).

S T. E. Hulme, *Speculations: Essays on Humanism and the Philosophy of Art*, ed. Herbert Read (London: Routledge, 1960).

SE T. S. Eliot, *Selected Essays*, 3rd edn (London: Faber, 1951).

SP Ezra Pound, *Selected Poems*, ed. T. S. Eliot (London: Faber, 1948).

UPUC T. S. Eliot, *The Use of Poetry and the Use of Criticism*, 2nd edn (London: Faber, 1964).

WLF T. S. Eliot, *The Waste Land: A Facsimile and Transcript*, ed. Valerie Eliot (London: Faber, 1971).

Most references to the above works appear within the body of the text.

1 Theoretical Preliminaries: Klein, Winnicott and Psychoanalytic Aesthetics

Sigmund Freud's early psychoanalytical theories were based upon his studies of hysteria and obsessional neurosis, and for all their subsequent expansion and mutation they continue to be marked, for both good and ill, by their origin in the analysis of the neuroses. This is no less true of Freud's ventures into aesthetics or literary criticism than it is of his more strictly professional work. His clinical experience of the psychoses was minimal and even his major paper on the paranoiac Schreber is based only on the Senatspräsident's autobiography.[1] He could accordingly never produce an adequate theory to explain the differential bases of the neuroses and the psychoses. The most significant developments in psychoanalysis outside the Freudian camp, however, have been grounded precisely in the study of psychosis, often carried out in mental asylums. For these more radical disturbances of the psyche, including schizophrenia, manic depression and paranoia, are characterised by a failure in reality-testing. Unlike the neurotic, the psychotic patient cannot know that he or she is ill; phantasy omnipotently invests the outside world and thereby becomes 'insanity'. Carl Gustav Jung investigated schizophrenia during his nine years as an assistant in a Zurich mental hospital (1900–9), and whatever personal factors were operative in his break with Freud in 1913, the antagonism is principally that between a theorist of the neuroses and a student of psychosis. Melanie Klein made still more important advances from the 1920s onwards by her pioneering studies of young children. Her thought has been developed in the British 'object relations' school of psychoanalysis, which has produced its most notable innovations in D. W. Winnicott's therapeutic work with borderline 'schizoid' patients.

It is this broad area of thought that I wish to explore for its suggestiveness for literary criticism and aesthetics. The work of Jung has of course been much canvassed, but, though as an analyst of psychosis he certainly has chronological priority, he seems to me too much a special case to merit extended discussion here. As one-sided in his own way as Freud himself, Jung too is unable to provide an inclusive theory that could map out the fixation points of both neuroses and psychoses; he simply has no interest in neurosis, relegating it to the level of the 'merely' personal, drearily unable to compete with the theoretical seductions of the 'collective unconscious'.[2] Moreover, in the study of modernist literature there is a nagging suspicion of circularity in applying the Jungian categories. Jung is himself so much a part of the moment of modernism, his thought so deeply marked by its pressures and distortions, that he can afford us no critical perspective on it. It is more profitable to read him alongside, say, Yeats and Eliot than it is to produce Jungian interpretations of the two poets' works. I therefore propose to turn to less 'compromised' psychoanalysts such as Melanie Klein and D. W. Winnicott.

Klein's work began with her analysis of children through her 'play technique', the interpretation of the child's free play in the analytic session as the symbolic dramatising of phantasies, the exploring and working through of anxiety, and her technique allowed her psychic access to very young children whose powers of verbalisation were minimal. But technical innovations in psychoanalysis already imply new theoretical departures, even if these are only fully articulated later, and so it was that Klein crossed swords with Anna Freud, who had also begun analysing children in the 1920s. Anna Freud's approach was strictly classical. Since the child was still emotionally dependent on its real parents, she argued, it would hardly 're-enact' in its relationship with the analyst the feelings and phantasies pertaining to those parents; there would be no transference neurosis because 'the old edition is not yet exhausted'.[3] The analyst's function should rather be educative than strictly analytical, aiming to strengthen the child's as-yet weak superego; and the superego is presumed to be weak because for classical theory it is a relatively late psychic acquisition. As an introjection of the parental prohibitions of the child's Oedipal wishes, it is a precipitate of the Oedipus complex, marking the dissolution of that conflict and the onset of latency. This Klein hotly contested. She argued that the Oedipus complex, far from emerging as late as the child's fourth year, was violently active at a much younger age, just as the superego itself was not the final product but rather the very earliest evidence of the complex. Her small patients, in terror of retaliatory attacks from persecutory parental figures, clearly revealed the operation of a primitive superego of remarkable ferocity. These *internal* figures led Klein to contest Anna Freud's claim that children underwent no transference neurosis, for it is the child's relationship to these inner phantasy figures (imagos) rather than the real parents that is projected onto the analyst, whose task is then not to reinforce a nascent superego, but rather to reduce the anxieties caused by the attacks of what is already a powerful and menacing agency.

In this primitive Oedipal situation the characteristic phantasies take *pre*-genital form, biologically rooted in the processes of oral introjection and anal expulsion (projection). Freud himself had noted that the superego is formed by introjection, but for him this remained only a curious anomaly, a regression to a primitive, cannibalistic mode of experience in the midst of the much later Oedipal material. It was precisely Klein's contribution, however, to demonstrate the quite fundamental importance of this early oral stage and of the child's relationship to the breast. It is true that the pre-genital drives are decisively inflected by the classical Oedipus and are only ever available in the adult subject as mediated by that complex, but by the same token the outcome of the Oedipus complex will be crucially affected by the pre-genital and pre-Oedipal configuration of the child's psyche.[4] It is therefore necessary to avoid a theoretical privileging of the early infant–mother relationship as one-sided as Freud's own investment in the full Oedipus complex. In what follows I have heavily stressed the importance of the pre-Oedipal and pre-genital, though never at the total expense of the classical Oedipus conflict, and this for two reasons. Polemically, because the question of the articulation of these two areas of psychic life in the literary text is hardly likely to be successfully addressed until the importance of the pre-Oedipal gains wider assent; no full balance can be achieved until that neglect is first redressed. Freudian psychoanalysis has had the literary-critical field so much to itself that its belated rivals are pitched – quite against their theoretical bent – into a fully Oedipal rivalry with their commanding precursor. But this emphasis on the pre-Oedipal also seems to me justified heuristically, because to focus on the Kleinian prehistory of the psyche will allow

a radical redirecting of attention to the poetry and drama of
T. S. Eliot.

I do not propose to give a diachronic account of Klein's thought,
which throughout the 1920s and 1930s is difficult and confused,
labouring to think new material in intractable Freudian concepts. It
is as if her play technique had thrown up such an astonishing
abundance of clinical material that the next decade or so had to be
spent assimilating it and developing the theoretical concepts that
would eventually organise it. It is therefore only a structural
account of the complete Kleinian system that confers on her early
work a teleology it so painfully did not possess at the time.[5]

Though I have pointed to Klein's breaks with classical theory, it
is none the less true that in some respects she remained truer to
Freud than did Anna Freud herself. As one of her defenders against
charges of 'deviation' from Freud shrewdly remarked, 'Mrs Klein's
"deviation" from Freud consists, in fact, of the radical
development of Freud's own greatest deviation from himself'[6] –
namely, the death instinct. For Freud that instinct is an ultimate
biological principle, a self-destroying desire to discharge the
instinctual tensions and 'unpleasure' of life so radically that the
organism returns to that lost Nirvana which is the inorganic; to
survive, the organism must deflect the death instinct into the
outside world and away from itself.[7] Klein accepts this account in
essence, but contends that there is sufficient human ego even at
birth to justify us in speaking of this primitive ego as *projecting* the
death instinct; this is no mere biological reflex but rather a human
defence against anxiety. The ego experiences the operation of the
death instinct as a fear of annihilation, as a threat to its still frail and
tentative organisation; and this is the fundamental anxiety which
remains active within all later forms of anxiety (even fear of
castration). Since there is an ego and not just an organism, the baby
is also already capable in Klein's view of very primitive *object*
relationships. The death instinct is thus not deflected into a void,
but rather projected into an object which at this stage can only be
the mother's breast; and this object, imbued with the child's own
destructiveness and sadism, is now felt as persecutory and itself
menaces the nascent ego. Part of the life instinct must accordingly
also be projected in order to create an ideal object, which will also
be the breast, and the ego will then seek to introject this ideal object
as a defence against the persecutory bad object. Both ego and the
object are now split into libidinal and destructive components. In

speaking of such defences as splitting, projection and introjection, I am already describing the area of psychic development that Klein formulated in 1946 as the 'paranoid–schizoid position'.[8]

Central to the description of the paranoid–schizoid position is Klein's concept of the 'internal object', of which the Freudian superego is only one example. Klein pushes the concept back into the very earliest months of infancy and describes the infant's relations to a whole series of *part*-objects, the mother's breast crucially, but also her hands and eyes, the father's penis, the child's own faeces and bodily organs. Though these objects have their origin in the external world, they are established as internal by a process of introjection. In this earliest stage of development the infant has not yet achieved a degree of reality-testing sufficient either to assemble the parts of bodies into structured wholes or to establish them as definitively 'not-me'. While external reality is coloured by the child's phantasies, it in turn reacts on them; phantasies of a bad and persecuting breast are reinforced by bad feeding experiences, as they are diminished by successful feedings. The quality of the (maternal) environment is therefore important for Klein, particularly in that the survival of the actual part-object or breast challenges the infant's destructive omnipotence and reinforces the good internal object on which the ego is ultimately founded.

If the infant must introject an ideal breast capable of yielding 'unlimited, immediate and everlasting gratification',[9] it must also cope with the assaults of the now-fragmented persecutors. The bad breast is at once shattered and invested by the infant's own oral, urinary and anal sadism, and Klein's stress on the sheer ferocity of the baby's relation to its mother's body retains a scandalousness that Freudian infantile sexuality has long since lost. It was a vision that initially appalled even her: 'the idea of an infant . . . trying to destroy its mother by every method at the disposal of its sadistic trends – with its teeth, nails and excreta and with the whole of its body, transformed in phantasy into all kinds of dangerous weapons – presents a horrifying, not to say unbelievable picture to our minds'.[10] But this repertory of destructive phantasies only ricochets back on the infant itself: the bad objects are introjected and form the persecutory superego. Bad environmental experiences increase the severity of the attack, and hunger or maternal absence may be felt as an annihilating invasion of persecutors. To deal with anxiety the infant mobilises a series of 'schizoid defences', including omnipotent denial, splitting, projection and idealisation, and these strategies seem to me essential in a psychoanalytic approach to the texts of T. S. Eliot.

Bertolt Brecht once remarked that he had 'never found anybody without a sense of humour who could understand dialectics', and, in a rather grimmer way, much the same is true of schizoid defences, of which indeed some of the finest examples are contained in the Hegelian master–slave dialectic.[11] Variously self-defeating, unravelling with one hand what it is busily concocting with the other, the schizoid strategy never quite sees that the joke is on it. Even projection, a fundamental mechanism grounded in the biological process of anal expulsion, does not 'resolve' its outcast impulse, which returns to plague the psyche from the outside. Rooted in the dualism of the instincts, splitting is no less fundamental, shearing away the negative from the positive aspects of a single ambivalent object; but the binary opposition is never as secure as the subject would like, and the sundered terms contrive a furtive embrace just out of the direct line of psychic vision. Idealisation plumps its object with a sudden access of libidinal energies only to discover its own miserable leanness and begin resenting its well-rounded partner; the object was to have tenderly nursed psychic energies from the persecutor, but it has stashed them away inside itself as spoils instead. Omnipotent denial finds itself fixated on precisely what it aimed to snub: by evading the anxiety that would prompt a deflecting of the psyche away from the feared object into the outside world, it remains stonily confronting an object it won't even admit exists. I shall later try to demonstrate both the alarming sadistic violence of Eliot's texts and this weirdly self-undermining 'humour' that haunts their every 'schizoid' gesture.

All these defences aim to evade anxiety, which is, however, a necessary spur to psychic maturity. They are disabling in proportion to their success, inhibiting 'symbol formation', the libidinal cathexis of the outer world that is the foundation of the child's relationship to reality:

> Since the child desires to destroy the organs (penis, vagina, breasts) which stand for the objects, he conceives a dread of the latter. This anxiety contributes to make him equate the organs in question with other things; owing to this equation these in their turn become objects of anxiety, and so he is impelled constantly

to make new and other equations, which form the basis of his interest in new objects and of symbolism.[12]

If, however, the initial anxiety which prompted the very first deflection from the mother's body to symbolic objects is avoided, the child remains in the severely retarded (autistic) relationship to the external world that Klein movingly evokes in her case study of a four-year-old boy who neither talks nor plays, and whose dismally impoverished relations to his environment consist of a vague interest in door handles and railway stations. If environmental factors are unfavourable and the schizoid defences mobilised to any great extent, the most severe psychopathology will result; adult psychosis derives from difficulties and fixations in this paranoid–schizoid phase.

In more favourable conditions the need to project bad impulses is less, anxiety based on persecution diminishes, the internalised good object and ego are more secure. As the split between ideal and persecutory aspects of the object (which is still, chiefly, the breast and mother's body) diminishes, the infant is now ready for the decisive recognition of the contradictory aspects of the *single* external object, or, subjectively, of his or her own *ambivalent* impulses towards that object. Reality-testing is developed to the point where the real object can be distinguished from the child's primitive phantasies, and this capacity is itself a result of a notable cohering of the ego. But we have now left the paranoid–schizoid organisation and entered the 'depressive position'.[13]

The mother is now perceived and loved as a whole person and, as such, introjected as a defence against continuing paranoid persecution; but, precisely in proportion as she defends, she also becomes vulnerable. Moreover, as a whole person, she is subject to the whole force of the child's ambivalence and no longer shielded by splitting and idealisation from the destructive impulse. As Winnicott will later suggest, she is resented for her very autonomy, hated for her overthrow of the child's cherished omnipotence. Under this combined assault by persecutors and the child's sadism, the introjected mother is shattered and the inner psychic world left a waste land of shreds and tatters. It is this desolation that prompts the label 'depressive', and in this position lie the fixation points of adult manic depression. Destruction of the internal object intensifies the old fears of disintegration of the ego, and the whole range of schizoid defences are once more summoned alarmingly into play.

But new feelings are also present, notably mourning for the lost object and, still more strikingly, guilt, as the child faces the realisation that its own aggression has caused this devastation. Whereas 'guilt' in the paranoid–schizoid position is primarily fear of retaliation from the persecutory superego, depressive guilt involves the more benign self-accusation signalled by the term 'conscience'. Guilt in turn gives rise to the crucial impulse of this phase, which is that of *reparation*, an effort to reconstitute into wholeness the dispersed fragments of the good object.

The infant mourns the lost object, and for Klein adult mourning is a derivative of this 'depressive' experience. Here she again differs from Freud, for whom the work of mourning was a long process of reality-testing in which the mourner must discover over and over that his or her lost love object no longer exists in the outside world. Klein argues that Freud does not explain why this process should be so painful. She suggests that any loss in adult life reactivates the agonies of the infantile depressive position; the loss of the external object, who has already been unconsciously identified with the fundamental parental introjects, throws into jeopardy the whole internal world. The work of mourning is accordingly one of introjection: 'The individual is reinstating his actually lost loved object; but he is also at the same time re-establishing inside himself his first loved objects – ultimately the "good" parents – whom, when his actual loss occurred, he felt in danger of losing too.'[14] But there is a danger of regression to paranoid–schizoid defences against the depressive pain, which may lead to a self-thwarting fixation and melancholia; the object must be allowed its autonomy and not subjected to the omnipotent manipulations of the primitive ego. The work of adult mourning and its psychic forbear, depressive reparation, are both an internal psychic labour and yet spill over into the objective world in the play and symbol formation of the child or the more complex symbolic activities that constitute adult creativity. The theory of reparation is thus the basis of the Kleinian accounts of art that I shall examine below. If the child can successfully restore the good internal object, securing upon it a firm organisation of the ego and a capacity for sustained reality-testing, it has in Klein's view negotiated the depressive position and is on course for 'normal' development. Later traumas may shake but cannot shatter the ego security founded here. Since for Klein the depressive organisation is the decisive *rite de passage* of human development, she consigns the affects of its paranoid–schizoid predecessor to the realm of the dangerous and regressive; her two theoretical terms do not peacefully coexist, but are structured in a violent hierarchy. It is this over-investment in the depressive position that is the major ground for dissatisfaction with Kleinian psychoanalysis, but rather than confront it directly I want to demonstrate how it is mined from within, how the very attempt to construct a Kleinian aesthetics subverts its own foundations in an ironic re-enactment of the self-molestings of a schizoid defence.

Klein's own interest in art found expression in her 1929 paper 'Infantile Anxiety Situations Reflected in a Work of Art and in the Creative Impulse'. Though written before she had formulated the notion of the depressive position, it none the less adumbrates a depressive theory of art which later Kleinian aestheticians have systematised. Yet the metaphor of 'reflection' and her fortuitous selection of items suggests that the analyst's relation to her material is both exploitative and opportunistic, more of a primitive manhandling than a delicately responsive reparation. Her paper is attractive not so much on account of its intrinsic merit as for the picturesque complement it provides to my excessively cryptic account of its author's psychoanalysis.

It is Colette's libretto to Ravel's *L'Enfant et les Sortileges* that affords a direct reflection of infantile anxieties in the artistic text itself. Since Klein has to narrate the libretto before she can analyse it, her procedure is open to an objection that can also be levelled at Freud's account of Jensen's *Gradiva*.[15] The problem is one of a self-confirming circularity; the initial narrating is a pre-processing of the work such that it then yields all the desired analytic conclusions without a murmer of dissent. None the less, the tale Klein tells is an entertaining one. A little boy is left by his mother who threatens, 'You shall have dry bread and no sugar in your tea.' In a fury he attacks the objects in the room around him, including a cat and squirrel. But the objects swell to monstrous size, and when he flees to the garden to escape their retaliation more cats and squirrels and owls prepare to attack him too. Safety is only achieved when, prompted by an impulse of pity, he nurses a squirrel injured in the struggle; at once the world resumes its normal size and becomes benevolent again. Nothing could be more Kleinian. Mother withholds the nourishing breast, and the child's attack on the room and its contents is a symbolic assault on her body and the phantasised riches it contains (father's penis, infant siblings); but the violence of his projections bounces back upon him and the objects are no longer victims but persecutors. Nursing the squirrel reveals the care for damaged internal objects characteristic of the depressive position, thereby marking the transition out of the paranoid–schizoid. No longer subject to the distortions of primitive phantasy, objects can at last be recognised in their otherness; they return to normal size as a result of successful reality-testing. This is pleasant allegory, but typical of early analytic criticism in its inability, which Freud himself often conceded in his interpretations, to illuminate the *formal* features of the work of art.

Infantile anxieties may be 'reflected' in the psychology of artistic creation, and the resourceful Klein finds a second example as curiously apt as her first. In a biography of the painter Ruth Kjar, it is noted that Kjar's artistic career began after the removal of a merely decorative picture from the wall of her room. For the intense depression that followed that event – the empty space 'grinned hideously down at her'[16] – intensified until in desperation she painted a life-size figure of a naked negress directly on the wall, the first achievement of her long professional career. The depressive reaction to the blank space relates to fears of the omnipotent destruction of the internal mother, and Klein argues that Kjar's painting is a symbolic re-creation of that mother and that depressive anxieties and their reparative urges are the source of artistic creativity. Or, rather, it remains unclear whether she is urging a theory of artistic creativity *as such* or simply illuminating the psychic processes behind works that are, more or less explicitly, representations of the mother's body. The very closeness of fit between instance and theory inhibits the generality of the latter. This difficulty recurs in the most recent attempt to apply Kleinian categories to art, Peter Fuller's *Art and Psychoanalysis*. In a fascinating analysis of the discovery of the Venus de Milo, Fuller charts the troubled, occasionally violent history of its passage to France and its proposed reconstructions. He argues that the nineteenth century's fascination with that fractured image must be seen in the light of Kleinian reparation, applied now to the artistic product rather than process. But the limitation of this account is precisely its brilliance as a *tour de dorce*; the work offers no challenge to the theory, but rather appears as a uniquely appropriate, one-off instance for it. No Kleinian writer escapes the schizoid, and Fuller's strength returns upon him as his own undoing. Though he will use the Kleinian defence mechanisms to extend his thesis to works of 'manic denial' like Hiram Power's *The Greek Slave*, the implication of the argument is that Kleinian psychology can be relevant only to works that represent the maternal body.[17]

This problem is addressed in one of the central statements of a Kleinian aesthetics, Hanna Segal's 'A Psycho-Analytical Approach to Aesthetics' (1952), reprinted in the 1955 collection *New Directions in Psycho-Analysis* alongside an equally seminal contribution by Adrian Stokes entitled 'Form in Art'. Dissociating herself from the Freudian attempt to reconstruct the artist's childhood conflicts from the symbolic content of the work, Segal complains that such an approach neglects precisely those features which constitute the work as an aesthetic object: formal organisation and the capacity to yield pleasure. She adheres to the Kleinian view of art as restoration of the good object, but cuts that process loose from the specific content of the work. If it makes reparation, it does so not by reconstructing a maternal representation, as Klein and Fuller imply, but by its formal structuring. Form as well as content may be the bearer of unconscious affect: it is in his or her loving attention to the formal resolutions and harmonies of the work that the artist engages in symbolic reparation, and the spectator's pleasure in the work's integration is itself an overcoming of depressive anxieties. Whereas content is destructive phantasy, form assuages, universalises, redeems. It is perhaps no mean feat to have rewritten the alarming extremism of her mentor's theory as banally as this. The stress on the restoration of a whole object through form is swiftly assimilated to familiar Romantic doctrines of the 'organic unity' of the work of art, and in a culture that equates women (especially the mother) with Nature the way is open for Segal's consoling conflation of organic form with the maternal body.

Adrian Stokes shares Segal's fetishisation of form, which constitutes 'a benign or unifying experience, however dire [the] subject matter'.[18] But at the same time the Kleinian position begins to crumble in his hands, for he aims, however diplomatically, to question the primacy that Segal gives to the depressive position and hence to art as reparation. Stokes intends to find a place in aesthetics for the 'oceanic' merging of self and other which Freud regarded as characteristic of mystical experience: 'we can always discover from aesthetic experience that sense of homogeneity or fusion combined, in differing proportions, with the sense of object otherness' (p. 414). He insists that form 'be conceived in terms of these two imagos' or prototypical experiences: oneness with a satisfying breast and acceptance of the mother as a separate person. While he concedes to Segal that the second imago 'possesses a temperate power' over the first unity with the breast – and we may wonder just how much of a concession his epithet amounts to – he none the less maintains that his first imago is no mere manic denial of aggression. Indeed, he is driven to postulate a distinctive 'Aesthetic position', situated somewhere between the predominantly manic defences and the normal depressive outcome, and this new 'position' 'uncovers a more creative role than usual for the manic defence mechanism: one that is potentially non-stultifying' (p. 416). Since, however, manic defences are by definition stultifying, it is clear that Stokes's intuitions are straining against the conceptual framework of Kleinian psychoanalysis and will only be adequately articulated outside that system. It seems that Stokes is labouring to convey what D. W. Winnicott was to term the 'potential space' between mother and infant, and I therefore move on to Winnicott's thought, reserving a fuller treatment of Stokes's psychoanalytic aesthetics for a later discussion of his relationship with Ezra Pound.

A paediatrician before he became an analyst, Winnicott generates his crucial theoretical innovations from his extensive clinical observation of mothers and newly born infants. Just as Klein's play technique had allowed her to excavate to deeper psychic strata than Freud's Oedipal analysis of Little Hans,[19] so Winnicott pushes back beyond even the Kleinian positions into the remotest prehistory of the psyche. One of his major stresses is the stunningly banal paradox that 'there is no such thing as an infant, meaning, of course, that whenever one finds an infant one finds maternal care, and without the maternal care there would be no infant'.[20] This comment reveals the transition in British psychoanalysis from the instinctual determinism of Freud and (to a lesser extent) Klein to a full stress on the importance of object relations, of an interplay between infant and maternal environment that is not solely a matter of instinctual gratification. One empirical index of this interplay seemed to Winnicott to be that class of infantile phenomena that he dubbed 'transitional objects': the bits of sheet that a baby pushes into its mouth, the handkerchief at which it may suck, the soft toy or doll to which it is passionately attached, all of which assuage anxiety or allow immediate sleep. These transitional objects belong neither to the realm of Oedipal interpersonal relations nor to the Kleinian world of internal objects, but rather allow Winnicott to propose an intermediate area between the subjective and that which is objectively perceived: the 'potential space' between mother and infant.

Such objects denote a transition between the earliest phase of primary identification where the baby makes no distinction between itself and the external world and that later phase in which the (maternal) environment is decisively repudiated as 'not-me', Klein's depressive position. Whereas for Klein and Segal the sense of seamless fusion of self and other is a manic idealisation designed to evade real aggression towards the breast, Winnicott merely points out, again from his paediatric experience, that fusion is in some sense a *fact* of infantile life:

> The mother, at the beginning, by an almost 100-per-cent adaptation affords the infant the opportunity for the *illusion* that her breast is part of the infant. It is, as it were, under the baby's magical control. The same can be said in terms of infant care in general, in the quiet times between excitements. Omnipotence is nearly a fact of experience. (*PR*, pp. 12–13)

Illusion it may be from the analyst's perspective, but in Winnicott's phenomenological psychoanalysis such fusion reveals its experiential ground. In more Freudian terms, even as biological need threatens the merging of self and environment the infant's hallucinatory wish fulfilment will coincide with the actual mother's feeding breast:

> the breast is created by the infant over and over again out of the infant's capacity to love or (one can say) out of need. A subjective phenomenon develops in the baby, which we call the mother's breast. The mother places the actual breast just where the infant is ready to create, and at the right moment.
> (*PR*, p. 13)

The mother's task is, however, to disillusion or wean her child, and the transitional object is itself a stage in this process; it is as significant for its *not* being the real breast as it is for being its substitute. It exhibits the same paradoxes as the original relationship to the breast, but also constitutes a rudimentary form of play, allowing the child to explore, dramatise and master this interface of self and other: 'It comes from without from our point of view, but not so from the point of view of the baby. Neither does it come from within; it is not a hallucination' (*PR*, p. 6). If the baby is now able to cathect an object both in addition to and as substitute for the breast, that is because the beginnings of disillusionment, the breast's affront to infantile omnipotence, have provoked the infant's destructive impulses and put into motion all the familiar Kleinian mechanisms. The breast now appears as persecutor, provoking in its turn the anxiety that leads the child to displace its interest onto the environment in the Kleinian process of symbol formation. Object-relations theory thus abandons the Freudian notion of a biological death instinct, explaining aggression rather as the consequence of frustrating relationships to objects: 'at whatever age a baby begins to allow the breast an external position (outside the area of projection), then this means that destruction of the breast has become a feature. I mean the actual impulse to destroy' (*PR*, p. 108).

Play, like the transitional object, also belongs to the interface of self and other that Winnicott terms 'potential space': 'the hypothetical area that exists (but can not exist) between the baby and the object (mother or part of mother) during the phase of the repudiation of the object as not-me, that is, at the end of being merged in with the object' (*PR*, p. 126). As Klein herself saw, playing is an interchange of phantasy and external reality, but she insufficiently emphasised that play itself is a therapy; it is therefore not so much the analyst's task to interpret the products of play as it is to remove those blocks and inhibitions that make this self-therapeutic process impossible. Far from being a merely instinctual process, play is actually impeded if instinctual excitement becomes too clamorous a component of it. Winnicott is urging a truly *free* play, and he points to the irony of Freud's 'free' association, which is in fact wholly determined by a psychic text written beforehand: 'free association that reveals a coherent theme is already affected by anxiety, and the cohesion of ideas is a defence organisation' (*PR*, p. 65). Winnicott's suggestion here is that the neurotic formation is itself only a symptom of (defence against) some more fundamental dissociation of the psyche. The condition of the child's play is a dissolving of the depressive ego into the 'potential space' between subjectivity and the external world, a dissolution only made possible by the child's paradoxical capacity to be 'alone in the presence of the mother'. The psychotherapist must recreate such conditions for the adult patient: 'a non-purposive state, as one might say a sort of ticking over of the unintegrated personality . . . formlessness' (*PR*, p. 64).

Winnicott's value for this study of the work of T. S. Eliot is his insistence that Klein's depressive position, the separating out of both object and ego, has its pathological aspect and may be carried to manic extremes where it denies both an aggressive relation to the breast and that more benevolent interplay that is the potential space. Hence Winnicott sides with Carl Gustav Jung rather than his mentor Klein in his reference to patients who are 'so firmly anchored in objectively perceived reality that they are ill in the . . . direction of being out of touch with the subjective world and with the creative approach to fact' (*PR*, p 78). For such Jungian 'extraverts' the therapeutic need is to retrieve the ability 'to become unintegrated, to flounder, to be in a state in which there is no orientation, to be able to exist for a time without being either a reactor to an external impingement or an active person with a direction of interest and movement'.[21] This inability to flounder is no surprise, since the rigidly suppressed subjective world is likely to be one of peculiar violence and contradictoriness involving all the features of the Kleinian paranoid–schizoid position. It is possible to get a long way in the analysis of Eliot's poetry and drama in terms of a dialectic between this extreme depressive separating out from the maternal object and the insistent return of the (paranoid-schizoid) repressed.

In later writings, Winnicott extends the notion of potential space from infantile phenomena to adult cultural activity, because any response to a work of art will involve a loosening of the boundaries of the ego and entail that indifferentiation of spectator and object that Adrian Stokes termed the 'Aesthetic position'. At the same time he redefines the infantile preconditions of potential space. Less a matter of the adaptation of the mother's breast to the baby's needs, though that will remain crucial, it now involves the mother returning the *gaze* of her feeding infant and establishing a beneficient circuit of exchange: 'What does the baby see when he or she looks at the mother's face? I am suggesting that, ordinarily, what the baby sees is himself or herself. In other words, the mother is looking at the baby and *what she looks like is related to what she sees there*' (*PR*, p. 131). Winnicott acknowledges his debt to Jacques Lacan's paper 'Le Stade du Miroir', but despite his wholesale importing of specular imagery the differences between the two analysts are more significant than Winnicott's bald comment that 'Lacan does not think of the mirror in terms of the mother's face' (*PR*, p. 130) would suggest. For Winnicott the mirroring gazes are

a primitive but fundamental form of the Hegelian 'recognition' that
Lacan acknowledges as the subject's demand for recognition by the
'Other'.[22]

But the Lacanian theory of psychosis is a more illuminating
parallel to Winnicott's. Anika Lemaire writes that

> The maternal attitude is determinant here. . . . If the mother
> treats her child as the complement of her own lack, as the phallus
> with which the child is in any case trying to identify, if,
> therefore, the child is everything to her and merges with her in a
> diffuse union, then the child cannot dispose of his own
> individuality. (*JL*, p. 234)

This is little more than Winnicott himself says in discussing the
developmental difficulties of 'the baby whose mother reflects her
own mood or, worse still, the rigidity of her own defences' (*PR*, p.
131). The infant is curiously neglected and appropriated at once,
encountering a bruising 'rigidity' which rebuffs its tentative gaze
but also being irresistibly smothered in a 'diffuse union'. But the
Lacanian emphasis on the baby representing the phallus for the
mother is valuable:

> when the mother denies the speech of the father its function as
> law, she prevents the child from acceding to the paternal
> metaphor, to the representation, that is, of a father who is the
> authority separating the child from its mother. Such an attitude
> leaves the child subjugated to the dual relationship, to
> identification with the mother, and takes from him any
> possibility of access to the order of symbolism and
> language. (*JL*, p. 235)

If the child is the complement of the mother's unconscious lack, it
is locked into what Lacan terms the 'Imaginary Order',[23] its access
to language radically impaired; and this, I shall argue, is the sorry
plight of J. Alfred Prufrock. Unlike Winnicott, Lacan points the
relationship between psychosis and language, and this will be of
particular relevance to a poet whose act of writing is at once
symptomatic and strategic in relation to these difficulties, scarred by
its psychic 'ruins' yet at the same time feverishly 'shoring' up its
linguistic fragments against them.

The representation of the 'phallic woman' in Eliot's poetry and drama has its meaning in this context. There is an Oedipal attempt to deny female 'castration' here, but its deepest resonances seem to me pre-Oedipal. Klein points out that in the infant's earliest phantasies the father's penis is kept within the mother's body, just one testimony among others of the teeming vitality of that body in its most intimate depths. But in Eliot the father never gets his penis back. The female body may seethe with forces, substances and secretions that threaten to burst forth upon the outside world, but, I shall argue, it has an ultimate principle of *retention* and its viscous energies will not finally abandon its warm interior. Folded away within the maternal body, the father will never emerge in Eliot as the fully Oedipal agent of prohibition. Lacan proposes the term ' "pre-Oedipal triangle" ' in order to designate the mother–child–phallus relation, the third term of which comes into play as the phantasy object of the desire of the mother'.[24] But the phallus is also the child itself, appropriated by the mother's imperious phantasy. In representing the phallus for her, he cannot accede to the 'paternal metaphor', cannot pass from the biological father to the 'Name-of-the-Father' as an abstract place of prohibition and law, a transition that would guarantee his own future occupation of that coveted role. This failure, result of the mother's unconscious phantasy, is conceived as a castrating attack by her; unable to possess the phallus in any full sense, the child feels that the mother has snatched it away altogether and stashed it away within her bodily interior. But he will determinedly prise open that body in its pursuit, and so it is, as Doris cries in *Sweeney Agonistes*, that 'A woman runs a terrible risk' (*CP*, p. 134).

2 Wrestling with the Devil of the Stairs: Early Poems to *Prufrock*

My reading of Eliot's work will be guided throughout by a maxim enunciated neither by Klein nor Winnicott but by Eliot's own imaginative creation, Sweeney. In *Sweeney Agonistes* the hero's relish for his narrative of a man who murders his mistress and keeps her body in the bath spills over into the excited generalisation that

> Any man has to, needs to, wants to
> Once in a lifetime, do a girl in.
> (*CP*, p. 134)

This claim may be turned back upon the poetry itself, for it will emerge that any Eliotic text has to, needs to, wants to, in one way or another, do a girl in; and if it fails to achieve that goal, it is itself murderously threatened by the girl. I shall argue later that this is indeed the case with *Sweeney Agonistes*: Doris may have drawn 'the COFFIN very last card', but the text is unable to dispose of her decisively, and it accordingly gutters out into silence, being consigned by Eliot to that section of his. *Collected Poems* headed 'Unfinished'. If the text cannot finish the girl, she threatens to finish it, and this danger is still clearer in the brief prose poem 'Hysteria', an emblematic text in the Eliot *oeuvre* which has received less than its due share of critical attention:

> As she laughed I was aware of becoming involved in her laughter and being part of it, until her teeth were only accidental stars with a talent for squad-drill. I was drawn in by short gasps, inhaled at each momentary recovery, lost finally in the dark caverns of her throat, bruised by the ripple of unseen muscles. An elderly waiter with trembling hands was hurriedly spreading a pink and white checked cloth over

18

the rusty green iron table, saying: 'If the lady and gentleman wish to take their tea in the garden, if the lady and gentleman wish to take their tea in the garden . . .' I decided that if the shaking of her breasts could be stopped, some of the fragments of the afternoon might be collected, and I concentrated my attention with careful subtlety to this end.

(*CP*, p. 34)

It has been suggested that the title refers rather to the speaker than to the woman. Impressed by the flagrant sexual symbolism of those rippling, unseen muscles, we may conclude with A. D. Moody that he 'is reduced to a state of nerves by her sexuality',[1] or rather by his own phantasy of a voracious and cannibalistic vagina. Yet the speaker's fears of fragmentation and loss of independent identity belong more to the fundamental disorders of psychosis than they do to such comparatively manageable neuroses as hysteria. If the text closes with a desperately self-absorbed concentrating of attention that recalls the rituals of obsessional neurosis – an absorption that had earlier emerged in the pointlessly meticulous precision of 'pink and white checked cloth' and 'rusty green iron table' – that is because, as Winnicott suggests, neurotic formations may themselves be defences against deep-seated psychotic anxieties. The ego's terror of dispersal is here held precariously in check both by its obsessional realism and by the desperate virtuosity of its imagery: 'until her teeth were only accidental stars with a talent for squaddrill'. The potential destructiveness of the teeth goes mercifully out of focus as the text parades its own stylistic *brio*, and the image achieves on a small scale what 'Hysteria' aspires to overall by bringing the scattering energies of its accidental stars back into the centripetal discipline of the parade ground. Metamorphosing the woman's teeth into harmlessness, the image celebrates its feat of linguistic dentistry by its brash typographic pun: 'acci-dental stars'. The text flaunts its stylistic mastery precisely because it is not the mere report of a psychic crisis that takes place 'elsewhere', but is itself, in the process of its writing, the very means by which its psychotic anxieties are fought through.

Neither reflection nor document of a pre-given psychoanalytic conflict, the text is rather an active *strategy* whereby those conflicts are (it hopes) contained and resolved. The Laforguian preciosity of 'Hysteria' at once rivets down the ego against the forces that threaten to overwhelm it and yet remains scarred by that conflict, its brittle wit an index of the cost and precariousness of the victory. 'Language in a healthy state presents the object, is so close to the object that the two are identified'; but in 'Hysteria' the very excess of signification quells the object, a condition that Eliot diagnosed in Swinburne as 'morbidity' of language (*SE*, p. 327). The phrase applies aptly to 'Hysteria' itself, as a 'morbid' or neurotic practice of writing ceaselessly buttresses the ego against the psychotic disintegration the woman menaces.

I have suggested that the underlying phantasy here is of the *vagina dentata*, but there is a danger of too swiftly and too narrowly attributing psychoanalytic significance to the text. The Freudian label does scant justice to the unexplained and riotous gale of laughter that is the woman's most alarming characteristic in this prose poem. For this woman is the most formidable presence in *Prufrock and Other Observations* precisely because she laughs, as opposed to 'La Figlia Che Piange', the languid society women of 'Prufrock' or the coyly exploitative heroine of 'Portrait of a Lady'. Sucking the narrator into its vortex, threatening the radical dispersal of subject into object, the woman's laughter has something of the explosively liberating potential of Bakhtinian 'carnival':

> power-structures are estranged through grotesque parody, 'necessity' thrown into satirical question and objects displaced or negated into their opposites. A ceaseless practice of travesty and inversion . . . rampages throughout social life, deconstructing images, misreading texts and collapsing binary oppositions into a mounting groundswell of ambiguity into which all articulate discourse finally stutters and slides.[2]

It is just such a 'riot of semiosis' that the woman's laughter threatens to precipitate, and, while the text narrowly succeeds in containing it, it can do so only by (as it were) articulating its discourse to the second degree, forging a style at once so brilliant and so brittle that it seems all the more vulnerable to a subsequent assault. The lady, however, threatens to expose the carnal underside of this decorous language, to hound into the light of day the originary and bodily metaphors it ignores in favour of the excessively intellectual figures it concocts. The effaced metaphor in 'involved' is thus regenerated in the all too physical engulfings and wrappings of the phantasy that follows. Under pressure from the woman, language 'regresses' from the intelligible to the sensible to the point where its most sedate terms seem to unfold a vision of that mutual interaction of bodies which is Winnicott's 'potential space'.

The power structure parodied and overturned here by the woman's carnivalesque laughter is surely that which Freud delineated as the social process of joke-telling in *Jokes and their Relation to the Unconscious*. For Freud the joke, like the Oedipus complex, involves a triangular structure: 'a tendentious joke calls for three people: in addition to the one who makes the joke, there must be a second who is taken as the object of the hostile or sexual aggression, and a third in whom the joke's aim of producing pleasure is fulfilled'.[3] Since the second person, the object of the joke's aggression, is the woman, jokes emerge as one of the power structures of patriarchy, and it is therefore all the more scandalous that in Eliot's text this structure is turned on its head. For the joke – whatever it is – is on the speaker and the elderly waiter, Freud's first and third persons, driving one into his obsessional practice of writing and reducing the other to a shambling and nonsensical buffoon. Not only does this female laughter deconstruct the binary oppositions of self and other, subject and object; it equally turns inside out the triangular structures of patriarchal authority in its own miniature version of Bakhtinian carnival. The generic indeterminacy of 'Hysteria' is itself another facet of this wholesale deconstruction; neither prose nor poetry, it too bears witness to the power of the woman's laughter to interrogate the dualisms into which the social world is structured. It is thus only fitting that the single laughing woman in Eliot should, in all her uproariousness, appear in his only prose-poem.

Mention of the waiter and the triadic structure of the text returns us to the psychoanalytic identification of the *vagina dentata* and the problems it raises. For it too readily collapses the oral, cannibalistic assault that 'Hysteria' records into the genital anxieties of the classical Oedipal complex, whereas the closing sentence of the text insists that the 'fragmentation of the afternoon' (and of the ego with it) is decisively connected with 'the shaking of her breasts'. What is at question here is a *pre*-genital relation to the breast in which the psychic mechanisms are those of the oral stage and in which the fixation point of adult psychosis is located. This does not preclude an Oedipal reading of the text, for Klein has emphasised that Oedipal phantasies begin in the very earliest, pre-genital phases of infantile life. But it does mean that the Oedipal anxieties are not necessarily to be thought under the sign of castration, just as the child's Oedipal jealousy is not initially directed at his or her parents' genital intercourse: 'according to the child's stage of libidinal development', Segal points out, 'he phantasies his parents as exchanging libidinal gratifications, such as mutual feeding and sucking at the oral stage or exchanges of urine or faeces or anal penetration at the anal stage'.[4] And the restaurant setting of 'Hysteria' testifies that the Oedipal phantasies involved here are indeed the exchange of oral gratifications. The text certainly reveals a tangled web of Oedipal ambivalences. If, as I have suggested, the speaker and elderly waiter are aligned against the disruptive laughter of the woman, it is also true that the waiter is a mere contemptible caricature set over against the more vivid figures of woman and narrator. The text contrives to push the father into a merely subsidiary role outside the charmed circle of mother and child: 'If the lady and gentleman wish to take their tea in the garden', he mutters, obligingly offering to absent himself from the Oedipal gratifications that would ensue. At the same time, however, the waiter is in some sense in collusion with the woman, since his evident discomfiture and absurdity are all grist to her hilarity; waiter and lady constitute a mutually reinforcing spiral of nonsense that only intensifies the narrator's terror of dissolution. Characteristically in Eliot the father is a dim, barely defined figure, present only at the remote fringes of consciousness; rarely does he attain his full Freudian stature as castrating rival for the mother's body. Oedipal anxieties are thus experienced in this text as that threat of the dissolution of the ego which Klein saw as the most fundamental human anxiety. Decisively inflected as it is by the classical Oedipal complex, this primitive anxiety is not thereby merely abolished, and I have argued above that there is a historical balance to be redressed in psychoanalytic criticism by foregrounding this anxiety against its better understood successor. But it is the relatively absence of the father in Eliot, prefigured by his marginal role in 'Hysteria', that affords the second justification of a largely pre-Oedipal and pre-genital approach, its simple appropriateness to the subject. For Eliot's poetry the classical Oedipus is less a starting-point than a goal yet to be reached.

The very method which the narrator of 'Hysteria' adopts to contain the menace of a splintering dissolution of the ego succeeds only dubiously. His aim may indeed be to collect the fragments of the afternoon, but his method of linguistic mastery, of stylistically cajoling the fragments into submission, leaves him further than ever from cohering them into a structured whole. He is left with a collection of brilliant *aperçus*, or of descriptive details whose very excess gives them a quality of phantasmagoric intensity that has more in common with the Kleinian paranoid–schizoid than it does with the coherent social world the ego is trying to restore. In a typical schizoid reversal the very energy that went into battening each object and detail down seems to return ominously upon the subject. The woman too is perceived in paranoid–schizoid fashion; she is a series of alarmingly autonomous part-objects – teeth, throat, breasts – that the shaken narrator cannot totalise. Far from being an isolated curio in the Eliot canon, 'Hysteria' adumbrates themes that are central to Eliot's poetry and defines the essential project of much of his work. '. . . if the shaking of her breasts could be stopped, some of the fragments of the afternoon might be collected. . . .' It is the rest of Eliot's verse and drama that will explore the viability of stilling those dangerous breasts, concentrating its attention with careful subtlety to that end.

It is only recently that the full range of materials necessary to trace Sweeney's theme of 'doing girls in' has become available. Eliot's *Poems Written in Early Youth* appeared in 1967, the facsimile of *The Waste Land* in 1971, and it was not until 1977 that Lyndall Gordan's *Eliot's Early Years* provided descriptions of a quantity of manuscripts that remain unpublished. Gordan locates the preoccupation with sainthood that marks many of these manuscripts and much of Eliot's published text in the tradition of New England Puritanism, as Eliot's repudiation of the bland Unitarianism of his parents; but her book owes its forcefulness less to this explicit thesis than it does to the powerful impression it conveys of the extremism and intense strangeness of Eliot's inner life, and I shall make frequent recourse to it both as a quarry of unpublished materials and as support for my own 'extremist' readings of Eliot's poetry.

In pursuing her theme of sainthood, Gordan observes how strikingly often Eliot's mother's poetry anticipated her son's in its themes and motifs; and how, like the domineering parents of her son's plays, who place the burden of justifying their lives on their children, Charlotte Champe Eliot sought oblivion for her own poetic failure in the prospect of her son's achievement: 'I hope in your literary work you will achieve early the recognition I strove for and failed' (*EEY*, p. 4). In his recent studies of poetic influence, Harold Bloom has charted the ephebe's Oedipal struggles with his paternal precursor, but his scheme of literary history has so far found no place for Eliot. May that not be because Bloom's own Oedipal anxieties alienate him from a poet facing a still more intolerable situation in which the ambivalent precursor is also the biological mother? Existentially fraught though that situation may be, it is none the less *theoretically* productive, for Eliot's texts thereby interrogate the polarities of contemporary feminist theory. Feminists like Luce Irigaray have argued that women live a more inward, unstable, bodily relationship to writing than do men; for the latter, deeply marked as they are by the phallus as 'transcendental signifier', signs are stable and ideal entities external to the body.[5] This, as we have seen, is true of 'Hysteria', where the woman unleashed the physical energies safely petrified in such an inert metaphor as 'involved'. But in Eliot the woman is also a wielder of signs, a suave rhetorician whose linguistic self-possession the poet can only envy and whose command of stylistic resource quells his own stuttering efforts at articulation; I shall argue later that this is the case in 'The Love Song of J. Alfred Prufrock'. As Bloomian precursor the woman incarnates an authority which she at the very same moment undermines in Irigarayan fashion: she thus eludes the literary-historical paradigms of the former even as she queries the patriarchal assignment of women to the irrational, which is merely revalorised in the feminist theory of the latter. In this sense, too, the neurotic practice of writing in 'Hysteria' may prove self-defeating. It reaffirms the ego in its stylistic narcissism only at the cost of engaging the woman on a terrain which, other texts assure us, she has already won in advance. While this study will not be a tracing of the anxieties of influence between the Eliot canon and *Easter Songs* and *Savonarola*, that may none the less be a necessary task in any future full evaluation of Eliot's poetry.

But Bloom has not merely ignored Eliot in his critical practice; he has consistently denounced him at the level of theory, particularly on the issue of tradition:

Since poets . . . idealise themselves, and their relations to other poets, there is already an excessive self-regard in poetic and critical tradition. Modern theories of mutually benign relations between tradition and the individual talent, including those of T. S. Eliot and Northrop Frye, have added their idealisations, so that it becomes an enormous labor to clear away all of this noble obfuscation.[6]

Arguing that mutual interplay is an idealisation evading the traumatic facts of aggression, Bloom resembles Hanna Segal in her insistence that the 'oceanic' merging of self and other that the work of art may invite is invariably a manic idealisation of the maternal breast that evades acknowledgement of aggression and thus reparation. It was against this view that Adrian Stokes proposed his makeshift notion of the 'Aesthetic position' and that the whole thrust of Winnicott's work has been more systematically directed. For Winnicott explicitly endorses Eliot's account of tradition and the individual talent:

> in any cultural field it is not possible to be original except on a basis of tradition. . . . The interplay between originality and the acceptance of tradition as the basis of inventiveness seems to me to be just one more example, and a very exciting one, of the interplay between separateness and union.　(*PR*, p. 117)

Bloom would no doubt agree with the first sentence, though it is not uttered in the tragic tone he would consider appropriate to such an observation. In contrast to his lineage of mutually castrating titans, Winnicott's notion of tradition is a *pre*-Oedipal one, an investment of affects whose distant biological root is the infant's most primitive interaction with the mother's body.[7] But, if Eliotic 'tradition' is not a manic idealisation as Bloom would have it, it is none the less precarious. The 'potential space' proposed in the first half of Eliot's 'Tradition and the Individual Talent' is soon disrupted by the disturbing psychic pressures of its second section, where the desired 'extinction' of personality is no fruitful interplay of subject and object, but rather the wholesale dispersal of the former into the latter which may indeed serve the same function as Segal's manic union with the breast.

In an interview late in life Eliot claimed that his poetry was American rather than English: 'in its sources, in its emotional springs, it comes from America' (*EEY*, p. 2). This is certainly true of two poems written in 1908 and 1909, 'Circe's Palace' and 'On a Portrait'. The former evokes a woman of sinister and violent eroticism; her fountain flows 'with the cries of men in pain', the petals of its flowers are 'fanged and red with hideous streak and

stain'. Lyndall Gordan aptly identifies Eliot's Circe with the
stereotype of the 'emasculating witch who . . . gathers strength
from Madeline Usher and Rappacinni's daughter, who radiate an
energy that Poe and Hawthorne regard as dangerous, perverse, or
abnormal' (*EEY*, p. 25). But the Homeric tradition is important
for the poem too, for it keeps open the tacit possibility that the
speaker is none other than Ulysses himself, the sole Greek capable of
overpowering this dangerous witch and subjugating her energies to
his quest to resume the roles of father and husband in Ithaca. By
means of the classical allusion the poem thus holds open beyond the
letter of the text an absent–present space where it achieves the
triumph it cannot sustain in the body of the poem itself.
Ambivalently poised between Circe and narrator in the lines on the
page, the python–phallus is ultimately guaranteed to the latter by a
silent narrative that hovers at the margins of the text.

Invocation of the *vagina dentata* in relation to Circe is more
appropriate than it was in the case of 'Hysteria'; the 'fanged' petals
are a genital image whose component of oral sadism is directed at
castration and not a more general dissolution of the ego. 'Circe'
seems, moreover, to be the first appearance in his verse of a
central Eliotic situation: the proposed ascent of a staircase at the top
of which awaits an ambivalently desired and threatening woman. As
yet Eliot has not put this situation into dramatic motion, but he
assembles its elements in a way that makes unusually clear their
psychoanalytical value:

> Along the garden stairs
> The sluggish python lies.
>   (*PEY*, p. 26)

As this phallic image indicates, the ascent of the stairs is a sexual
penetration into the female body, and in the 'sluggishness' recorded
here we have an anticipation of the 'hundred visions and revisions'
that assail Prufrock as he contemplates a related ascent. At the same
time the python is associated with the fanged flowers, panthers and
peacocks which are all aspects of the alarming energies released by
Circe; and to that extent, far from constituting an aggressive
penetration into her, it is already her own possession. In contrast to
the more glamorous panthers and peacocks, however, the
sluggishness of the python pointedly refers to the Homeric Circe,
who in transforming men into hogs effected a particularly graphic

making over of the intelligible into inert materiality. In terms of the phallus it would seem that the woman thus blocks the child's access to the paternal metaphor: disabled by some stratagem of Circean magic from separating the Name-of-the-Father as empty, abstract place from the physical father himself, the male child can then not accede to that future role. He remains wallowing on Aeaea instead of returning as father to Ithaca.

The garden stairs are as ambivalent as the python that occupies them. The staircase affirms distance between poet and woman but none the less offers the consolations of communication (the stairs could always be mounted), while in asserting their interconnection it also preserves a discreet and saving separateness (the stairs have not yet been mounted and need not be); everything is thus possible but nothing actually undertaken, a situation whose ironies J. Alfred Prufrock will savour. Moreover, the garden stair asserts an essential disparity between poet and Circe, which will re-emerge later in Eliot as that between infant and idealised, omnipotent mother or, alternatively, between self-abasing masochist and domineering mistress. If the poem phantasies an incestuous penetration into the body of the mother, it also knows the cost of that gratification to be castration, a threat which comes not from the father but from Circe herself. The lurid horror with which she is evoked compacts both the Oedipal prohibition and the more primitive phantasy of the persecuting breast which underlies the images of cannibalistic sadism; the panthers of 'Circe's Palace' are distant precursors of the leopards who devour 'my legs my heart my liver' in *Ash-Wednesday* (*CP*, p. 97). Inflected by the classical Oedipus complex, this primitive oral imago remains fearfully potent none the less.

Eliot's evocation of the evanescent, pensive goddess of 'On a Portrait' completes the stereotypical juxtaposition – woman as sinner or saint – that Gordan locates in the tradition of American Gothic as charted by Leslie Fielder in *Love and Death in the American Novel*. Eliot commented obliquely on this tradition in his late essay 'From Poe to Valéry', where, after dismissing the substance of Poe's poetry as adolescent, he admired its incantatory style, which 'because of its very crudity, stirs the feelings at a deep and almost primitive level' (*CC*, p. 31). This recalls his earlier discussion of the 'auditory imagination': 'the feeling for syllable and rhythm, penetrating far below the conscious levels of thought and feeling, invigorating every word; sinking to the most primitive and forgotten, returning to the origin and bringing something back'

(*UPUC*, pp. 118–19). Later, in 'The Three Voices of Poetry', Eliot referred approvingly to 'Gottfried Benn and his unknown dark *psychic material* – we might say, the octopus or angel with which the poet struggles' (*OPP*, p. 100). If the poet's struggles recall Harold Bloom's *agon* with the poetic precursor, then Eliot's description of the antagonist – octopus or angel – coincides with the split representations of women in his earliest poetry, as of American Gothic generally. Poe's value to him was perhaps less purely formalist than he was inclined to allow.

This association of Eliot with American Gothicism at the start of his career is one way of loosening his poetry from its conventional categorisation with the Symbolist tradition. At the other end of that career Eliot attempted his own extrication of his work from that lineage. In 1947 he announced the demise of *poésie pure*, and six years later in 'The Three Voices of Poetry' he recommended an account of poetic composition by the German Expressionist Gottfried Benn. No longer is the mind of the poet an inert shred of platinum, it is rather 'haunted by a demon, a demon against which [the poet] feels powerless, because in its first manifestation it has no face, no name, nothing; and the words, the poem he makes, are a kind of form of exorcism of this demon' (*OPP*, p. 98). Freed from its subservience to the Symbolist tenet of the autotelic, unparaphrasable work of art cut loose from psyche and history, criticism might at last attend more fully to the dramas of subjectivity that Eliot's texts fight out. Eliot's citations from Benn point towards his affinity with the probing of extreme, even pathological mental states characteristic of European Expressionism, and I shall develop this link further in my account of *The Waste Land*. But the youthful relationship to Gothicism is a no less salutory reminder of all those aspects of Eliot that consort uneasily with the rarefied heritage of Mallarmé and Valéry, and suggests that these psychic dramas may be analysed in terms of the Jungian archetypes, as Fiedler recommends, or more fruitfully (it seems to me) in terms of the Kleinian internal objects.

In the Laforguian poems of 1909 and 1910 the dual aspects of the woman are presented in toned-down but still recognisable form. 'We deny our Symbolist Masters, the last Moon-lovers', exclaimed that arch anti-feminist Marinetti,[8] but these texts by Eliot are under the sway of just such a lunar imago. His dandyish protagonist is condemned to wait 'on the doorstep of the Absolute', and the capitalised abstraction looks forward to Eliot's imminent involvement with the neo-Hegelianism of F. H. Bradley. What prevents that ascent in 'Spleen' is perhaps the formidable female companion of 'Conversation Galante', who is apostrophised as 'The eternal enemy of the absolute' (*CP*, p. 35). The 'mad poetics' of this latter text bears upon the issues I have raised in relation to 'Hysteria', for the fluent periods of this conversationalist are in fact evidence of a radical linguistic insecurity. Whimsical and leisurely, the poem parades an unruffled surface of signifiers; but, as it concedes in its self-referential account of the moonlight nocturne, it is merely bodying forth its own vacuity. This musical image implies that language is no more than a keyboard at the speaker's disposal, passive until subject to his virtuoso manipulations, whereas from another viewpoint this style is virtually autonomous, casting up one image after another even when the speaker attempts to detach himself from them ('fantastic, I confess') and thus halt the process. The principle of digression that the woman notes is not just a contingent failing but rather the very substance of the style itself. Laforguian irony then allows the poet to acknowledge and evade this in a single gesture: the virtuosity of the master rhetorician becomes a matter of being haplessly open to every linguistic breeze that blows, of achieving, as he claims the lady does, an 'air indifferent and imperious' at once.

The woman's own utterances, clipped and laconic, plumped full with and in stable relation to intended meaning, give short shrift to the poet's maundering ascent to the Absolute, but they do not altogether cow him. So corrosive is the text's irony that it infiltrates even these self-assured dicta, downgrading them to the mere obtuseness of a society hostess who cannot follow the poetic reveries of her interlocutor; and this is a stratagem Eliot will employ again in 'Prufrock'. The woman's deflationary technique gives 'our vagrant moods the slightest twist', and the verbal anticipation of 'the last twist of the knife' in 'Rhapsody on a Windy Night' is no accident (*CP*, pp. 35, 28). The witty cut-and-thrust in the 'Conversation' becomes the brutal stabbing of Romeo in 'Nocturne', which leaves him rolling 'toward the moon a frenzied eye profound' (*PEY*, p. 29). This all-pervasive moon has, of course, such traditional connotations as female chastity and purity; 'La lune ne garde aucune rancune' (*CP*, p. 27) because it is an idealised breast, one from which all destructive aspects have been split off. But the moon may also symbolise Cybele, castrating moon-goddess, and the text's efforts to introject the good breast, to ascend the doorstep, are accordingly thwarted by its counterpart, the bad sexual breast. Droll and off-hand as they are, these Laforguian poems are none·the less playing for high psychic stakes, and the unease that mines their formal assurance finds its substantive expression in the figure of the bloodied Romeo.

The dualistic representations of woman recur in Eliot's 'Rhapsody' and are never folded back into the 'lunar synthesis', the recognition of ambivalence towards a *single* object, that the poem initially promises. Under the midnight moon 'every street lamp that I pass / Beats like a fatalistic drum', and this image, coupled with the murderous violence of the madman towards his dead geranium, casts a sombre shadow over the 'dull tom-tom' hammered out in the protagonist's brain in 'Portrait of a Lady' (*CP*, pp. 26, 19). If the moon is as much ironised as idealised in the 'Rhapsody', its sexual counterpart nevertheless emerges with unusual explicitness as the lurking prostitute of its second stanza. Here too the imagery leads outwards: the corner of the prostitute's eye 'Twists like a crooked pin' (*CP*, p 26), recalling the no less piercing eyes of the women in 'Prufrock':

> The eyes that fix you in a formulated phrase,
> And when I am formulated, sprawling on a pin. . . .
> (*CP*, p. 15)

The appearance of the whore 'throws up high and dry / A crowd of twisted things' (*CP*, p. 26), but this psychological associationism only obscures the element of phantasised oral attack that runs through the next twenty lines of the poem. A branch eaten smooth upon the beach, the cat devouring a morsel of rancid butter, the crab remorselessly gripping the end of a stick – images of orality and aggression that circulate around the presence of a forlorn child. 'I could see nothing behind that child's eye' (*CP*, p. 27): its gaze frozen into opacity, this child knows nothing of the rich interchanges of the potential space. Even its gestures of play are furtive and futile:

> So the hand of the child, automatic,
> Slipped out and pocketed a toy that was running along the quay.

Here, clearly, it is not the products of play that are in need of a Kleinian interpretation, but rather the *process* of play itself that needs freeing from the blocks and inhibitions that keep it at this dismally impoverished level. Located at the exact mid-point of the text (lines 38–40 of a seventy-eight line poem), this moving image of a child stunted in its symbol-formation is the centre around which the paranoid–schizoid phantasies of the poem organise themselves. The 'whispering lunar incantations' that open the 'Rhapsody', like the incantatory rhythms of Poe's poetry, 'because of [their] very crudity, stir the feelings at a deep and almost primitive level' (*CC*, p. 31), gaining access to the dark areas where the Kleinian octopuses and angels lurk. For Eliot's philosophical mentor F. H. Bradley, 'our experience when relational is not true',[9] and in dissolving 'clear relations, / Its divisions and precisions Eliot's 'Rhapsody' hints at the deep psychoanalytical waters that underlie its author's involvement in Bradley's dialectic. Dissolving the protocols and formalities of the more familiar social world where poems like 'Prufrock' and 'Portrait of a Lady' are, however precariously, located, 'Rhapsody on a Windy Night' constitutes the dark underside of those more decorous texts. If, as I shall suggest below, there is an absent centre to 'The Love Song of J. Alfred Prufrock' – the vanished 'Pervigilium' – then Eliot's 'Rhapsody' may be considered a strong candidate for that unfilled office.

In the summer of 1910 it seems that Eliot achieved the Absolute he desired: 'while walking one day in Boston, he saw the streets suddenly shrink and divide'. Thus Gordan paraphrases 'a poem he never published called "Silence" his first and perhaps most lucid description of the timeless moment' (*EEY*, p. 15). The immediate antecedents of this revelation are of some interest. Inspired perhaps by Arthur Symons's *The Symbolist Movement in Literature*, Eliot was already planning to go to Paris after graduation from Harvard, a decision his family bitterly resisted. For the Unitarian imagination Paris was an unspeakable and festering corruption: 'I cannot bear to think of your being alone in Paris, the very words give me a chill', his mother wrote.

> Eliot held out against this opposition, but in May went down with a mysterious illness. He was hospitalised with suspected scarlet fever and his mother rushed to Boston. It was not serious, but it prevented him from taking his final examinations that spring in comparative literature, fine arts, and French. (*EEY*, p. 33).

A 'mysterious' illness that destroys the chance of academic attainment in precisely those fields most closely connected with his family's condemnation of Paris's artistic decadence bears all the marks of a neurotic symptom. Since Eliot broke down in May and wrote 'Silence' in June it is likely that his mother's dash to Boston and his renewed dependence on her during convalescence were the immediate basis of that vision of the still point.

The difficulties of interpretation here are obvious: 'Silence' remains unpublished, the biographical information is meagre, and I do not anyway intend my readings of the poems to rest on psychobiography. But there may be a suggestive parallel with Wordsworth's experience of

> those obstinate questionings
> Of sense and outward things,
> Fallings from us, vanishings

in the 'Ode: Intimations of Immortality'. In his discussion of the poem, Lionel Trilling aptly cites Freud's account of the 'oceanic' feeling:

> a feeling which embraced the universe and expressed an inseparable connection of the ego with the external world . . . it would coexist like a sort of counterpart with the narrower and more sharply outlined ego-feeling of maturity, and the ideational content belonging to it would be precisely the notion of limitless extension and oneness with the universe.[10]

If the Boston streets shrink and divide, it may have been owing to just such a resurgence of oceanic idealism. Eliot's illness affirmed omnipotence as well as dependency in relation to the mother, imperiously summoning her to the place where her child's helpless needs were to be met, in a replaying of Winnicott's description of their early interaction. Restored after protracted antagonism to the supportive maternal environment, Eliot may thus have recovered the primitive oceanic relationship to the mother, of which 'Silence' in turn may be a celebration.

Whether or not this mystical experience was indeed a recovery of something like the potential space between mother and infant, it was very short-lived. Eliot carried out his intention to move to Paris (a move that involved such puzzling features as the resolve to abandon English for French and a change, which still awaits expert interpretation, in the very character of his handwriting), and within months those persistent octopuses were at him again: 'in his first blasphemous poem [. . . March 1911] God appears to be a sexual monster, a degenerate female who entraps her victims . . . an Absolute with arbitrary powers sitting in the middle of a geometric net like a syphilitic spider' (*EEY*, p. 39). Without a beneficent environment – the nursing mother – reassuring the subject that his destructive phantasies are not omnipotent, there a swift regression to the persecutory terrors of the paranoid–schizoid position.

Eliot's next poems included 'Portrait of a Lady' and 'Prufrock', and, as has often been pointed out, these texts should be seen in the light of his long and intense involvement in the philosophy of F. H. Bradley. Eliot began studying philosophy in the Harvard Graduate School in late 1911 and finally completed his doctoral dissertation, 'Experience and the Objects of Knowledge in the Philosophy of F. H. Bradley', in 1916. But this interest in Bradley should in its turn be seen in the light of Eliot's deep fascination with mysticism. Gordan has documented the impressive extent of Eliot's reading in mysticism and the psychology of religious experience. His chief complaint against his Harvard department was its divorce of philosophy from religion, and in seminars he defended the specificity of religious experience against anthropological reductions. Whereas Freud revealed the biological root of much religious emotion in the infant's ambivalent relation to the father, object-relations psychoanalysis has stressed the grounding of specifically *mystical* experience in the very earliest stages of the infant's relation to the mother, in Winnicott's potential space or Freud's 'oceanic' realm. We might therefore expect to trace within the turgid mass of Eliot's thesis on Bradley the submerged contours of this primitive relationship. Indeed, we might turn Eliot's comment on Ruskin back on himself and say that, 'whereas Bradley, like Newman, is directly and wholly that which he is', 'one feels that the emotional intensity of *Knowledge and Experience* is partly a deflection of something that was baffled in life'.[11]

Bradley is the chief English neo-Hegelian, and I therefore wish to bring to bear on Eliot's discussion of him Herbert Marcuse's suggestive account of Hegel in *Eros and Civilisation*. For Marcuse, *The Phenomenology of Spirit* unfolds 'the structure of reason as the structure of domination'. The developing self-consciousness is engaged in a twofold struggle: an attempt to subdue the material world which must become the means of its self-realisation, and a still more fraught effort to win recognition from another self-consciousness. Since this second ego takes the first as mere object, thus negating its very quality as self-consciousness, both are pitched into the life and death struggle which is the master–slave dialectic. Yet Hegel's philosophy 'would not be the self-interpretation of Western civilisation if it were nothing more than the development of the logic of domination'. For it also postulates a freedom that is the overcoming of the antagonistic relation to the other and the world, a state of the indifferentiation of subject and object. Because Being is then no longer a painful transcendence towards the future under the yoke of the Reality Principle but rather a blissful recapture of the past, 'remembrance here appears as the decisive existential category' of Hegel's thought.[12] Marcuse associates Hegelian remembrance with the Freudian Pleasure Principle, the discharging of instinctual tension by omnipotent and hallucinatory wish fulfilment, which occurs before the ego is sufficiently developed to deal with tension by adaptive behaviour. It will now, I hope, be clear how this relates to object-relations psychoanalysis, for, as Winnicott points out, such omnipotence is a *fact* of infantile experience:

> The mother, at the beginning, by an almost 100-per-cent adaptation affords the infant the opportunity for the *illusion* that her breast is part of the infant. It is, as it were, under the baby's magical control. . . . Omnipotence is nearly a fact of experience. The mother's eventual task is to disillusion the infant, but she has no hope of success unless at first she has been able to give sufficient opportunity for illusion.   (*PR*, pp. 12–13)

I propose, then, that Hegel's Absolute amounts to the recovery of this infantile omnipotence in relation to the mother, as Hegel's own stress on remembrance would indicate. Alienated from a primordial unity, cast into a universe of negativity, adrift in a world of opaque and antagonistic monads, the ego flounders desperately until it at last recuperates the lost potential space.

While Bradley's own system is not to be simply equated with Hegel's, it is none the less clear how powerful a grip the Hegelian paradigm of unity–alienation–redemption has over his thought. Bradley stands out among the Idealists of his time by his uncompromising insistence that the ego is not ultimately real, a contention so ideologically scandalous that in 1902 eight Oxford dons launched a philosophical broadside against it in a volume entitled *Personal Idealism*. In denying the reality of relations ('our experience when relational is not true'), Bradley committed himself to monism, the view that reality is one and indivisible and not a number of particulars related to each other: 'In the beginning there is nothing beyond what is presented, what is and is felt, or rather is felt simply. There is no perception of difference or likeness. There are, in short, no relations and no feelings, only feeling.'[13] As the biblical resonance of the opening words intimates, it is psychological depths that are being dredged here, not epistemological counters shuffled. But while 'feeling' or 'immediate experience' is the ultimate fact of Bradley's philosophy, it is also 'self-transcendent': shot through with a fundamental instability, it inevitably crystallises out into the familiar world of selves, relations and objects. We are always on the wrong side of a philosophical Fall for Bradley, which is by no means a 'fortunate' one; and the task of metaphysics is our (theoretical) redemption in the Absolute:

> the non-relational immediate felt unity, which is Immediate Experience, prefigures the supra-rational unity of the Absolute, in which thought and its object are united to form Truth, and the difference between the two stages is that, whereas in the former, divisions and relations have not yet emerged, at the latter, they have been transcended, they merge again in the highest experience.[14]

Immediate experience thus collapses into the dualisms of subject and object only to be recuperated at a point of full self-consciousness in the identical subject–object that is the Absolute. Just so, for Hegel, did the unreflective unity of individual and society in the Greek city state dissolve into the world of self-estrangement, only to be recaptured in the fully self-aware 'reconciliation' of citizen and state achieved by the French Revolution. For the narrative of unity–alienation–redemption is, as M. H. Abrams has persuasively demonstrated in *Natural Supernaturalism*, one of the most deep-rooted paradigms of Western thought; and in its aspirations towards an identical subject–object it represents a Utopian wish for the recovery of that indifferentiation of self and (maternal) environment that is Winnicott's potential space or, in another psychoanalytical register, Jacques Lacan's 'Imaginary' Order.[15]

In the broad lines of his own philosophy Eliot follows Bradley, yet he has radical doubts about his mentor's faith that the primordial Eden of immediate experience can at last be regained. The consoling appearance of the Absolute in Bradley's system offered an illusory satisfaction that Eliot scorned: it 'satisfies only an imaginary demand of feeling. Pretending to be something that makes finite centres cohere, it turns out to be merely the assertion that they do.'[16] He argued that Bradley had seriously underestimated the theoretical problems involved in reabsorbing everything into a higher unity, and that in particular he had paid too little heed to the recalcitrance of the 'finite centres' into which immediate experience had crystallised. This is the burden of the well-known passage from *Appearance and Reality* which Eliot appended to *The Waste Land*: 'My external sensations are no less private to myself than are my thoughts and feelings. In either case my experience falls within my own circle, a circle closed on the outside; and, with all its elements alike, each sphere is opaque to the others which surround it' (*CP*, p. 86). Eliot's difficulty is termed by him solipsism, though this is not solipsism in its usual sense of the claim that all experiences are mine alone. The existence of other selves is not denied, but the possibility of their ever establishing a common world is; the sheer multiplicity of viewpoints offers no hope of a final Hegelian synthesis. As Richard Wollheim has pointed out, this problem was made all the more intractable for Eliot by his peculiarly impoverished concept of mind. There were, he argued, no mental contents distinct from objects, or rather every apparent mental content was actually an object. 'However, by insisting more strongly than Bradley that we "arrive at objects . . . by meaning objects", that every object that a finite centre apprehends is real, Eliot has, to a correspondingly greater degree, the problem how to unite the different points of view into a single world.'[17] If Eliot denies the possibility of a resplendent synthesis, it is because he is rather less attached to the narrative schema of a fall from grace. Several of his poems will suggest that the apparently primordial state of grace was always already fallen, that it is not to be recuperated because it was never in any full sense there in the first place.

It seems a long way from the abstruse reaches of Bradleyan metaphysics to Sweeney's enthusiasm for 'doing girls in'; and yet

Eliot's curious juxtaposition of passages from Matthew Arnold and Bradley in his essay on the latter suggests that it may not be. 'Anyone who is at all sensitive to style will recognise the similarity of tone and tension and beat'; but what is striking about Arnold's purple passage is its utter lack of anything that could even remotely be called 'tension and beat':

> And yet, steeped in sentiment as she lies, spreading her gardens to the moonlight, and whispering . . . the last enchantments of the Middle Age, who will deny that Oxford, by her ineffable charm, keeps ever calling us nearer to the true goal of all of us, to the ideal, to perfection.   (*SE*, pp. 446–7)

In the wash of sentiment here we may detect an idealised maternal imago, an Arnoldian wish to lapse out into an infinitely protective mother. These lines typify Arnold as laureate of the 'buried life', that deliciously vague area of subjectivity dissipated by the alarms and struggles of an 'iron time'; and to recall the former phrase is also to recall Eliot's use of it in 'Portrait of a Lady'. For the heroine of that poem is, like Arnold's Oxford, an 'adorable dreamer, whose heart has been so romantic! who hast given thyself so prodigally', all too prodigally for the poem's curtly self-possessed narrator. It is, in contrast, the lines from Bradley that have all the tension and beat, particularly in their striking final image: 'Our principles . . . no more *make* that Whole which commands our devotion than some shredded dissection of human tatters *is* that warm and breathing beauty of flesh which our hearts found delightful.' '. . . some shredded dissection of human tatters': this might be the fate of a patient etherised upon a table or of the terrified epileptic who watches Sweeney test the razor on his leg, just as 'tension and beat' themselves might describe the young man's 'soul stretched tight across the skies' in 'Preludes' (*CP*, p. 24).

These are cryptic suggestions and will, I hope, become clearer in the course of this study. At the moment I intend them only to hint that the images in question here are central to some of Eliot's major poems, for the juxtaposition of Arnold and Bradley creates what is virtually an Eliotic poem in its own right. Just as Eliot is less sanguine than Bradley that the dispersed chaos of finite centres can ever be folded back into the unity of the Absolute, so too is he unconvinced that the dissection of human tatters can be restored to its warmth and breathing beauty. If there is a phantasised attack on the woman here, it provokes not Kleinian reparation but a manic idealisation like Matthew Arnold's, which denies that the act of aggression ever took place at all. The images and psychic concerns of Eliot's poetry thus break through the decorous surface of a general assessment of Bradley, reversing the curious intrusion of *Appearance and Reality* into *The Waste Land*, for we are here at the very interface of philosophy and psychoanalysis. The note to *The Waste Land* informs us that 'every sphere is opaque to the others which surround it'. While it would be merely fanciful to speculate that those opaque spheres, like the moon–Absolutes of the Laforguian poems, are the now unresponsive maternal breasts, a more disciplined Kleinian interpretation might still be possible.

With the emergence of consciousness or the ego the pristine unity which is immediate experience is fractured, divided into the twin poles of subject and object. This process and the psychic defences it provokes can themselves be organised around these two poles. In so far as it is the object that resists the subject's omnipotence, breaking up the oceanic indifference of self and other by affirming its autonomy in face of the infant's unanswered need, it becomes the target of all the subject's frustration and sadism. With the object split into good and bad aspects, the latter is projected, but its destructiveness then returns upon the subject in persecutory form, and as defence against these new-found tormentors the infant must attempt to introject the good breast as the rock of defence of the ego. It was this tripartite struggle that I traced in Eliot's Laforguian exercises, where the introjection was never successful in face of the persecutors; baulked by the 'eternal enemy' (*CP*, p. 35), the poet waits disconsolately 'on the doorstep of the Absolute' ('Spleen', *PEY*). This failure is itself a consequence of the fact that introjection is not unambivalent in the first place. It may secure the ego from assault, but then the existence of the ego was itself a large part of the problem. Looked at from the pole of the subject, immediate experience disintegrates with the emergence of the ego, a process dependent upon the introjection of the good breast. As I shall argue later, Eliot's work contains a fierce streak of masochism, which arises because the ego itself becomes the target of the death instinct. That instinct is no blind and self-satisfying rage but rather the psychic expression of what Freud termed the Nirvana Principle: the longing for a final discharge of the subject's instinctual tensions, a release from the frustrations of dualism in the authentic, if Pyrrhic, unity which is the inorganic. With the mention of Nirvana it is timely to recall Eliot's sustained interest in Eastern religions, which culminates in his use of Sanskrit in *The Waste Land*. Like Bradley's immediate experience, Sanskrit is a primal and unified origin from which a host of particulars, the Indo-European vernaculars, have crystallised; and Eliot's poetry is inclined to share Bradley's view that our (linguistic) experience when relational is not true.

All this suggests that the dissolution of the ego which threatens in 'Hysteria' is not only feared; more 'positively', it offers a way back to the identical subject–object, which is the Absolute. Obliteration of either subject or object will do: mutually implicated as they are, the destruction of the one will also be the unravelling of the other. Eliot's texts accordingly have a reversibility that is a function of their psychic ambivalence. Violence against women is always potentially directed at the self, just as, in reverse, suicide for Freud was a defence against aggression directed at another.

Ambivalence can be 'overcome' by an extreme idealisation of the good breast and an omnipotent annihilation of persecutors in an effort to retrieve unproblematically the unity-in-duality of Winnicott's potential space; and this manic strategy, I shall argue later, is characteristic of Eliot's religious verse. But it can be more properly overcome only if acknowledged, if the splitting of the object ceases and it is recognised in its autonomy and contradictoriness. With this shift into the depressive position, guilt appears and impulses of reparation are mobilised. When *Prufrock and Other Observations* was published in 1917 with the dedication 'For Jean Verdenal, 1889–1915, mort aux Dardanelles', it declared itself a work of mourning, written under the provenance of the depressive ego. I have referred above to Klein's account of the work of mourning. It is no longer, as with Freud, a matter of painful reality-testing, but rather an effort to reconstitute the inner world thrown into jeopardy by the loss of an adult love-object who is always in part identified with the fundamental parental introjections. The danger in mourning is then of a regression to paranoid–schizoid defences against the depressive pain; the object must be respected in its integrity and otherness, not subjected to the omnipotent manhandlings of the primitive ego. Eliot's epigraph to the volume points to just these issues. Statius confesses to Virgil that he longs to 'treat the shadows like the solid things', and this may be taken as expressing a desire to move out of the world of indistinct part-objects that is the paranoid–schizoid position into

the more solid and coherent world of depressive reality. At the same
time, however, Statius concedes the vanity of his longing (he and
Virgil are, after all, only insubstantial spirits), and Eliot too will
never succeed in decisively shifting to a depressive mourning.

The world of J. Alfred Prufrock is clearly a paranoid–schizoid one,
composed of shadows rather than solid things. Whether he muses
in his room or sets out through half-deserted streets remains unclear;
there is insufficient differentiation between inner and outer for any
reality-testing to take place. Objects do not exist independently and
in their own right, but are already assimilated to Prufrock's
subjectivity. This is not a universe of significant otherness involving
three dimensional space, but rather the 'flat world of changing
lights and noise' to which the simple soul issues forth in 'Animula'
(*CP*, p. 113). Just as in that later poem there is an inability to make
objects cohere into wholes, so too in 'Prufrock' such objects as are
discerned are typically part-objects: hands that lift and drop a
question on your plate, arms that are braceleted and white and bare,
eyes that fix you in a formulated phrase. It is less a specific woman
than these intimidating part-objects that are Prufrock's concern in
the text. As there is no sense of objective space, so there is none of
time; past, present and future coexist. 'Should I´ . . . have the
strength . . .' Prufrock ponders prospectively, but eight lines later
concedes, 'I was afraid', as if the crisis were a determinate past
event (*CD*, pp. 15–16); such temporal dislocations are
characteristic. Prufrock even proposes his own theory to explain
them.

> Is it perfume from a dress
> That makes me so digress?
> (*CP*, p. 15)

It is proximity to the female body that ruptures narrative
continuity: not only can the alarming fragments of that body not be
totalised, but one's relationship to it cannot be given the reassuring
shape of a teleology.

Both space and time are collapsed into the all-encompassing
simultaneity of the Bradleyan finite centre, and in the context of
this paranoid–schizoid world Prufrock's oral fixation can come as
no surprise. The fog is imaged as licking its tongue into the corners
of the evening; Prufrock himself yearns to spit out all the butt-ends
of his days, longs to bite off the matter with a smile, wonders if he

dares to eat a peach, and knows that if he ever does gain the
strength to force the moment to its crisis it will only happen after
the oral debauch of 'tea and cakes and ices':

> I should have been a pair of ragged claws
> Scuttling across the floors of silent seas.
>   (*CP*, p. 15)

This is not, as Hugh Kenner argues, 'too good a couplet to sacrifice
. . . though it appears to belong to another, unwritten poem',[18] but
is rather the summation of this vein of imagery, an unusually
explicit phantasy of bristling oral sadism. It is, moreover, typically
paranoid–schizoid in its fragmenting of the whole crab into just
claws and scuttle.

This mode of fragmented perception is, I suggested,
characteristic of Prufrock's relationship to the woman, whose own
pair of arms lying along a table is a curious complement to the
ragged claws. In *Eliot/Language* Michael Edwards has suggested
that the claws image is over-determined since 'a crab moves
sideways, like a writer's hand. And the image is not two pairs of
claws but a single pair, the thumb and fingers of the poet gripping
his pen.'[19] If this is indeed so, then the awkward, hurried
movements denoted by 'Scuttling' hint at how little at ease
Prufrock is in this medium, and his earlier 'hundred indecisions . . .
visions and revisions' may be the measure of just how fraught his
access to language is (*CP*, pp. 15, 14). He is no more assured in
handling the very grain of his medium than he is in manipulating its
larger narrative structures. Scuttling, revising and digressing, his
lines lurch towards inarticulacy, fade out into *points de suspension*, or
founder, restart and yet again lose direction. 'It is impossible to say
just what I mean!' Prufrock cries frustratedly (*CP*, p. 16): meshed
in the toils of language, he dreams, like T. E. Hulme and Imagist
poetry, of a mode of verse that would 'hand over sensations bodily'
(*S*, p. 134), 'as if a magic lantern threw the nerves in patterns on a
screen (*CP*, p. 17). Prufrock's painful and partial articulacy is in
striking contrast to the women of the text who effortlessly
discourse of Michelangelo and possess the gift of the lapidary
'formulated phrase' (*CP*, p. 15). This is a wholesale reversal of
'Hysteria', where it was precisely the speaker's stylistic virtuosity
that was his major defence against the riotous pre-linguistic
laughter of the woman.

Prufrock's woefully incomplete possession of language recalls
Anika Lemaire's account of psychosis: 'when the mother treats the
child as the complement of her own lack, as the phallus', the child
remains trapped in the dual relationship, unable to accede to the
'paternal metaphor', robbed of any possibility of access to the order
of symbolism and language (*JL*, pp. 234–5). Small wonder then
that Prufrock should see himself as a decapitated John the Baptist –
my head . . . brought in upon a platter' (*CP*, p. 16) – presented to
the formidable Salomé, for this image of castration testifies to his
defeated acquiesence in the appropriative phantasy of the mother.
Forced to represent the phallus for her, he cannot possess it in any
full sense himself and is to that extent castrated. It is at just this
moment that Prufrock sees 'the eternal Footman hold my coat, and
snicker'. The Footman is at once the realm of the Father, snickering
contemptuously at a subject lamely unable to resist the mother's
phantasy and thereby confined to the psychotic margins of the social
order, and another version of the nonsensical waiter in 'Hysteria', a
father figure himself reduced to marginality by a formidable
woman. In his ambivalence the Footman both proclaims the value
of all that has been lost and provokes the subversive doubt that it
would not have amounted to much after all, for the text is at least
as inclined to celebrate as it is to lament its fixated bond to the
mother.

This fraught relationship to the mother is foregrounded in the
later 'Hamlet' passage. This paragraph was considered a blemish by
Ezra Pound, the censoring father-figure of Eliot's early verse, but
Eliot clung to it with unusual tenacity; it was, Pound wrote, 'an
early and cherished bit' which 'T. E. won't give up'.[20] Eliot's
attachment to the lines may have appeared a little less perverse even
to Pound when the former later devoted one of his most intriguing
critical essays to 'Hamlet and his Problems'. There he described
Hamlet as 'full of some stuff that the writer could not drag to light,
contemplate or manipulate into art' (*SE*, p. 144), and this
unmanageable 'stuff' was for Eliot decisively associated with
Hamlet's relationship to his mother. 'No!' exclaims Prufrock, 'I
am not Prince Hamlet, nor was meant to be' (*CP*, p. 17); but
negatives in poetry are oddly powerless, testifying by their very
resistance to the compelling force of that which they supposedly
cancel, and the writer's only satisfactory mode of negation is
erasure. We may thus ignore Prufrock's caveat and consider the
value the figure of Hamlet has for him. His exclamation succeeds

his phantasy confrontation with the woman and thereby points its own relationship to Hamlet's decisive encounter with his mother in Act III, scene iv. There it is the task of the Prince to persuade his mother to submit to the law of the father by foregoing sex with Claudius, just as it is his own duty to accede to his father's vacated role by avenging his death; and in neither of these aims is he unequivocally successful. Prufrock, however, is cowed by the mere prospect of challenging the woman, hence the intensity of his denial that he is Hamlet and the frenetic metonymic displacement whereby he scuttles along a chain of *dramatis personae* – attendant lord, Polonius, Yorick the Fool – to distance himself as far as possible from the Prince. But the energy here arises at least as much from repulsion as it does from mere timorousness. It is not only Hamlet's daring in undertaking to subdue Gertrude, but that very enterprise itself, that appals Prufrock; the verse paragraph does not simply fail but actively *flaunts* the law of the father by just being there in the first place. The text may concede its castration at the hands of Salomé, but it will yield nothing to the literary mutilations of an Ezra Pound, maintaining instead a tenacious grip on this 'early and cherished bit'. Even as it dolefully admits its inability to resist the appropriative mother, the Hamlet passage thus delivers a rebellious blow at the demands of his own literary father figure, thereby achieving something of the status of a Freudian compromise formation. The relationship with the mother is privileged as well as resented, and this small compositional skirmish with Pound is one instance of a wider confrontation over these issues whose ramifications I shall explore more fully in a later chapter.

It has often been pointed out that Prufrock displays a regressive yearning towards infantile sleep: the fog curls in slumber about the house, the evening malingers stretched on the floor, and at the close of the poem Prufrock himself dozes in the chambers of the sea 'Till human voices wake us' (*CP*, p. 17). But, as that final phrase intimates, such fulfilment remains a Utopian impossibility while female gazes 'fix you in a formulated phrase' (*CP*, p. 15), while they retain their fixed and dismissive opacity. It would seem that Prufrock has read his Winnicott, for, if the mother's unconscious preoccupations prevent her from returning the infant's gaze, the ontological confidence necessary to that relaxing of the ego which is the potential space or, later, adult creativity may never be attained. If Prufrock exists subjectively as a radically inchoate personality, the obverse of this is the rigidly curtailed and constricting social persona he compliantly adopts, the face he prepares to meet the faces that he meets. Winnicott describes the preliminary therapeutic stage for patients locked within the 'finite centre' as 'a non-purposive state, as one might say a sort of ticking over of the unintegrated personality' (*PR*, p. 64), which is not the alarming psychotic dispersal which the poem as a whole manifests; and Prufrock might well image this desired recovery of the potential space as a blissful lapsing out into infantile sleep.

I have suggested that the pair of ragged claws is not only a sadistic response to, but also a persecutory version of, the pair of arms that lie along the table, and such parallelisms and reciprocities may be traced elsewhere in the poem. There is the 'simple pin' of line 43 (*CP*, p. 14) whose firm assertiveness gives momentary stability to Prufrock's dandyish elegance and, more crucially, to his timorous ego. Fourteen lines later the woman's gaze has turned his own image devastatingly back on him as he finds himself 'pinned and wriggling on the wall' (*CP*, p. 15). The objects and images of this psychotic universe are terrifyingly unstable, bolstering the subject one moment only to turn viciously on him the next. Each image can be turned inside out to reveal its opposite: John the Baptist may have been hapless victim of the castrating Salomé, but Lazarus was only resurrected as a result of Mary and Martha's imploring of Christ. Scratch the surface of a Kleinian octopus and you are likely to discover an angel, and *vice versa*. There will be time, Prufrock cries, to 'murder and create' (*CP*, p. 14), but in this text aggression and idealisation turn out to be bewilderingly interchangeable. The good and bad imagos haunt the poem, but it is never entirely clear which is which. Nowhere is this more true than in the closing lines:

> We have lingered in the chambers of the sea
> By sea-girls wreathed with seaweed red and brown . . .
> (*CP*, p. 17)

The mermaids wreathe Prufrock as consolingly as the fog curled about the house, an idealised phantasy which defers, however precariously, the moment of 'human' waking and drowning. Yet such wreathing has something in common with the more alarming engulfings or 'in-volvings' of 'Hysteria', and the enigma 'Prufrock' leaves us pondering, eloquent by its very silence, is the mermaids traditionally drown their lovers. Danger does not loom from outside, but is in fact implicit in this phantasy Eden from the very start.

Prufrock fails to articulate his 'overwhelming question' (*CP*, p. 13), and this failure has been interpreted as a sign of Eliot's poetic tact (to specify a question is to make it less than overwhelming) and as symptomatic of the evanescent and self-deluded mind of the protagonist. But the failure may actually correspond to a failure of the poem's own, and in place of the missing question I propose we ponder the blank manuscript pages of the text: 'The rest of "Prufrock" . . . was copied into the Notebook, in his spiky hand, in July–August 1911. But Eliot deliberately left four pages in the middle of the poem blank' (*EEY*, p. 45). This absent centre was later titled 'Prufrock's Pervigilium' and it was apparently cut on the advice of Conrad Aiken (who denies this). All that Gordan reveals of the contents of this suppressed section is that it records an all-night vigil in which Prufrock hears the chatter of his own imminent madness and which climaxes in a horrifying vision of the end of the world. The poem was thus to have been a study of a much more radically disturbed personality than its present Laforguian veneer might suggest. This curious fragment of textual history seems to me to give support to a claim which Leo Bersani enunciates in his study of Baudelaire as a general interpretative principle of psychoanalytic criticism: 'no text is ever fully present to itself. There is a fantasmatic supplement, an absent extension of itself which a text never explicitly articulates but incessantly refers to, which it makes imperative only, as it were, by the high visibility of significant lacks.'[21] I would accordingly suggest that behind 'The Love Song of J. Alfred Prufrock' there lurks the occluded presence of a murderous narrative that may well be the emotional centre of Eliot's early poetry. It cannot be focused in this poem alone, but the initial image of the patient etherised upon the table may stand as its emblem. Commentary has endlessly rehearsed the 'deflationary' effect of this image upon the romance of sunset, but has never yet remarked that the patient is about to be or perhaps already is carved open by the surgeon's scalpel, a fate I have already intimated in pointing the parallel with Bradley's 'shredded dissection of human tatters' (*SE*, p. 447). Insensible and awaiting the surgeon's incision, Prufrock's patient is only a homelier version of those phantasies of bodily dismemberment whose Lacanian significance Allon White has described: 'Corporal disintegration is the reverse of the constitution of the body during the mirror phase, and it occurs only at those times when the unified and transcendent ego is threatened with dissolution.'[22] Typically reversible, the patient is at once Prufrock himself disintegrating into psychosis and also his victim, object of the repressed phantasy I shall now attempt to examine.

This 'fantasmatic supplement' is most resoundingly absent–present in the white space that separates the third from the fourth of Eliot's 'Preludes', a poem that prominently features the dual maternal imagos. An unspoken narrative links the fates of a yellowing woman dozing in her room and a (young?) man striding through the city streets, and the turbulent energies that that narrative releases explode into the paranoid–schizoid *tour de force* that constitutes the two final stanzas of the text. The 'infinitely gentle/Infinitely suffering thing' (*CP*, p. 25) curls around the sordid images as deliciously as the sea-girls who wreathed Prufrock, yet, unlike those mermaids, is not ambivalent; this infinite gentleness rather looks forward to the intercession of the Virgin Mary in Eliot's later verse. The good internal object is indeed idealised, but splitting is more successful here than ever it was in 'Prufrock', and the bad breast is expelled into the following stanza. The ancient women who drift through vacant lots testify to a successful phantasy attack on the bad object, torn to pieces and fragmented in a triumph of oral sadism. 'Wipe your hand across your mouth, and laugh', declares the text jubilantly, and the source of this manic energy is the silent transition between stanzas and personae at the end of Prelude III.

'It seems unnecessary to connect this terror of the stairs [in "Prufrock"] with Eliot's reading of *Crime and Punishment* in Paris', comments Hugh Kenner.[23] On the contrary, it seems to me essential to do so. When an American scholar suggested to Eliot that 'Prufrock' was deeply marked by his reading of Dostoyevsky, the poet agreed: 'These three novels [*Crime and Punishment, The Idiot, The Brothers Karamazov*] made a very profound impression on me and I had read them all before *Prufrock* was completed.'[24] Kenner points out that the motif of the terrifying staircase also occurs in 'Portrait of a Lady', written before Eliot went to Paris, and I have noted some of its features in 'Circe', which was completed still earlier. This hardly matters. If Dostoyevsky, and *Crime and Punishment* in particular, made such an intense impression on the young Eliot, it was because it articulated at once a narrative structure he had been fumbling towards himself for several years: a young man ascending a staircase to murder a woman. Just as Raskolnikov's detested old money-lender is a fitting candidate for the role of bad internal object, so the idealised prostitute Sonya Marmeladov corresponds to the good object. Raskolnikov butchers the former and wins the latter's love, and, as the 'ancient women' and the 'infinitely gentle . . . thing' of 'Preludes' testify, this is precisely what the poet himself achieves:

> His soul stretched tight across the skies
> That fade behind a city block,
> Or trampled by insistent feet
> At four or five or six o'clock . . . .
> (*CP*, p. 24)

The paranoid terror of these lines seems excessive as a notation of the pressures of urban existence, but appropriate to the newly blooded murderer. In the first the latent image of a racked and tortured body is a more gruesome version of the etherised patient of 'Prufrock'; skyscapes somehow lend themselves peculiarly to both Eliot and some of his Imagist contemporaries for this sort of projection of destructive phantasies.[25] It is also fitting that the third line has been noted as a reminiscence of the subterranean ravings of the murderous hero in Tennyson's *Maud*.

The religious overtones only a few lines later may again recall Dostoyevsky's novel, but they fit uneasily into my account of the poem so far:

> The conscience of a blackened street
> Impatient to assume the world.
> (*CP*, p. 24)

Eliot's praise of *The Changeling* in his essay on Middleton is relevant here:

> it is the tragedy of the not naturally bad but irresponsible and undeveloped nature, caught in the consequences of its own action . . . the unmoral nature, suddenly trapped in the inexorable toil. . . . Beatrice is not a moral creature; she becomes moral only by becoming damned [and] the possibility of that frightful discovery of morality remains permanent.
> (*SE*, p. 163)

These words, which also have a bearing upon *Crime and Punishment*, record access to the depressive position; the sudden discovery of morality is the ego's attempt to face the consequences of its own aggression. But comparison of the impersonal precision of Eliot's description of Beatrice with the 'frightful discovery' of conscience in 'Preludes' suggests how precarious guilt and reparation are in the latter. An 'impatient' conscience is already rather less self-effacing than it perhaps ought to be, a little too masochistically eager to shoulder the penance imposed, and 'assume' then bears upon us in its adjectival sense as 'overweening'; and there is anyway a bizarre overestimate of self implicit in the very notion of assuming the world, a feat fitting only for Messiahs. This is no less true if 'assume the world' is taken to indicate an impatience to escape the solipsism of the paranoid–schizoid position and posit the independent existence of objects. For the instability of 'assume' undermines this depressive aspiration too: it is less a question of conscience assuming in humble fashion a world that is already given than of its brashly arrogating its raw materials to its own subjective ends by idealist fiat. 'Conscience' is accordingly flawed and fragile in the text, and it could hardly be otherwise when the destructive phantasy that was to be acknowledged is as thoroughly repressed as it is here. A mere two lines after its mention of conscience the poem has regressed to the paranoid–schizoid position, and the psychic omnipotence implicit in the ambition to assume the world becomes the psychotic jubilation I have already described.

In his discussion of Middleton Eliot is skirting his central theme of sainthood, though in reversed form as damnation. Earlier, in the satirical sketch 'Eeldrop and Appleplex', he had been less cautious: 'In Gopsum Street a man murders his mistress. The important thing is that for the man the act is eternal, and that for the brief space he has to live, he is already dead. He is already in a different world from ours. He has crossed the frontier.'[26] Carve your mistress as you would a patient etherised upon a table and you are well on the way to beatitude: this is not a path to the Holy City Saint Augustine would have approved. Eliot once remarked of Baudelaire that 'he was capable of a damnation denied to the politicians and the newspaper editors of Paris' (*SE*, p. 429). That may be so: what is certain is that on his way to his spiritual destination (at least on the way as defined by T. S. Eliot) he would have provided ample and sensational material for those very newspaper editors. The murderous ascent of the staircase is thus Eliot's debt to

Dostoyevsky, and long remains central to his poetic imagination. While critics have discerned elements of this pattern before, it has not, as far as I know, been systematically examined in the light of the post-Freudian developments in psychoanalysis that seem peculiarly fitted to do justice to it. For the murdered woman is never simply one's mistress, but is first and foremost recipient of unconscious phantasies pertaining to the most primitive stages of the infant–mother relationship.

Two more poems in Eliot's first collection are relevant to these themes. There is, first, 'Portrait of a Lady', which has been much admired for the nuanced Jamesian ironies signalled by its title. But, in tracing these, criticism has had systematically to neglect the poem's epigraph from Christopher Marlowe's *Jew of Malta*, because the tonal and syntactic intricacies of a Henry James consort uneasily with the 'farce' – 'the terribly serious, even savage comic humour' – which for Eliot is Marlowe's 'most powerful and mature tone'. The juxtaposition of title and epigraph points to unruly, 'savage' pressures that will ruffle the poise of the poem's Jamesian narrator, and the nature of these psychic forces is further illuminated by the dramatic context of the epigraph. Barabas may well admit to the minor charge of fornication since he comes fresh from his criminal masterpiece: the poisoning of an entire convent of nuns. It is then scant surprise that among Eliot's touchstones of the mature Marlovian style, whose effect depends on 'always hesitating on the edge of caricature at the right moment', we should find:

> At last the soldiers pull'd her by the heels,
> And swung her howling in the empty air . . . .
>
> We saw Cassandra sprawling in the streets . . . .
> *(SE*, pp. 123–4)

Marlowe's account of the sack of Troy in *Dido* Act II, scene i, lodges in Eliot's memory as a set of 'savage comic' images of attack on women, just as *The Jew of Malta* is condensed to Barabas's poisoning of the convent. Nor is this atypical. Eliot may have recommended the extinction of individual personality by sinking oneself into the 'mind of Europe', but in practice, as I shall argue more fully below, the European mind seems to throw back only a swollen reflection of one's own deepest concerns. Here, at least, the poem's epigraph alerts us to the possibility of a kind of reading that its Jamesian title would at all costs deny.

The 'Portrait' begins with the 'atmosphere of Juliet's tomb' (*CP*, p. 18), an image hardly more auspicious than Prufrock's etherised patient awaiting the surgeon's knife. The four wax candles in the darkened room stake out a space for a woman's corpse, and the lady will indeed be dead – at least in the narrator's imagination – by the end of the poem. But the Shakespearean reference is also misleading; this is no youthful Juliet but rather a woman 'about to reach her journey's end' (*CP*, p. 20). Given the disparity between the ages of lady and narrator, a more apt Shakespearean comparison might well be Hamlet's encounter with his mother, and with that parallel in mind it is worth pointing the keenly felt autobiographical element here. 'And so you are going abroad; and when do you return?' (*CP*, p. 21): at the time he wrote this poem Eliot must have been fearing precisely these questions from his own mother. Unlike in the *Hamlet* scene, however, it is here the woman, not the young man, who makes the emotional running, pressing through social velleities to the more naked encounter that she assumes will 'somehow recall / My buried life' (*CP*, p. 20). That phrase itself recalls Eliot's descriptions of the poetic process as 'sinking to the most primitive and forgotten' (*UPUC*, p. 119) where the Kleinian octopuses and angels breed, for the lady is gesturing to the psychic forces crucial to his poetry. If the buried life is indeed the pre-Oedipal, then the stuttering repetitiveness of the lady's speech is rather more than the feather-brained meanderings of a society hostess. The Oedipalisation of the female is always less successful than that of the male, her access to the Lacanian 'Symbolic', the order of language, always more precarious. Hence it is that the lady's discourse, in a manner that recalls Prufrock's, is again and again on the point of lapsing away only to be set in motion once more by a juddering lurch forwards:

> And how, how rare and strange it is, to find
> In a life composed so much, so much of odds and ends . . .
>
> (*CP*, p. 18)

The slow, grinding violence with which she twists the lilac-stalks may be taken as, among other things, both an index of the psychic cost of, and a smouldering resistance to, patriarchal law and language, and thus constitutes a miniature instance of the alienating process graphically illustrated in François Truffaut's film *L'Enfant*

Sauvage, 'in which language learning comes before us as a racking torture, a palpably physical kind of suffering'.[27]

Yet the text is clear, as the lady is not, that there can be no simple withdrawal from the alienating circuits of language into the pre-Oedipal, for the relationship she offers the young man is precisely that: a regression to the self-enclosed bond between mother and son which Lemaire noted as the site of later psychosis. Poignant in the dignity of her isolation, the lady is at the same time ruthlessly manipulative towards the narrator in her effort to appropriate him as the phallus, as the complement of her own lack. But there can be no withdrawal. In the broken-backed line quoted above there is thrown up for our ironic contemplation the momentary syntactic unit of 'a life composed so much': cut away for an instant from its predicate, 'composed' bears upon us here in an alternative sense – 'written'. Even the image which records the ache of subjection and revolt against social constraint – 'slowly twisting the lilac stalks' (*CP*, p. 19) – itself reveals the lady as ineluctably written by a social text which exceeds and escapes her. Thirty lines earlier she had urged that the intimacies of Chopin

> Should be resurrected only among friends
> Some two or three, who will not touch the bloom
> That is rubbed and questioned in the concert room.
> (*CP*, p. 18)

But, far from constituting a privileged enclave of subjectivity beyond social determination, the hushed intimacies of personal encounter are ironically scored across by the very metaphor which evokes trivialisation within society. There can be no stepping back to a virginal pre-Oedipality, even if the young man would oblige, since there is no 'bloom' that is not always already rubbed and questioned. Even the lady's affirmation that the April sunsets 'somehow recall / My buried life' (*CP*, p. 20), reveals these ironies: to 'recall' is at once to revive and to revoke, a remembering but also an annulling.

'You will write, at any rate', remarks the lady gloomily (*CP*, p. 21), and the comment has a resonance and truth beyond her immediate intention. Like the speaker of 'Hysteria', this young man seeks to orchestrate a massive textualisation of human existence, transforming every last untidy fragment of it into 'the comics and the sporting page' (*CP*, p. 20). At the suggestion that he might write to her, his 'self-possession flares up for a second' (*CP*, p. 21). Writing is his defence against the woman, and that this is so reveals how wrong she is about her youthful interlocutor: 'You are invulnerable, you have no Achilles' heel' (*CP*, p. 20). Dipped by his mother Thetis into the river Styx so that the heel by which she held him was not immortalised, Achilles may serve as emblem of the fact that Oedipalisation (at least in Eliot's texts) is never wholly successful; and the young man too bears the far from defunct trace of the pre-Oedipal. His very stress on 'self-possession', on respecting the otherness of the object, is his oblique tribute to the strength of an impulse towards the indifferentiation of self and other, for the poem's peculiar achievement is to make of Klein's depressive position a manic strategy. The speaker separates himself off so decisively from his object that he can deny both his urge towards that which she offers and the destructive response her appropriative strategy simultaneously provokes. Aggression can accordingly enter the poem only in the form of its Marlovian epigraph or as the 'dull tom-tom' (*CP*, p. 19) that his brain menacingly beats. If Prufrock might be said to be 'ill in a psychiatric sense because of a weak reality-sense', the protagonist here is one of those apparently more secure characters that Winnicott describes as 'so firmly anchored in external reality that they are ill in the opposite direction of being out of touch with the subjective world' (*PR*, p. 78).

Writing will be the young man's way out of crisis, and his problem here is parallel to the text's own. The more 'written' it can be, the more it cultivates the infinite nuance of Jamesian cadence and syntax, the better chance it has of keeping its grotesque Marlovian epigraph firmly outside its elegant boundaries and of reducing it to an authorial *jeu d'esprit*. Yet both text and hero face a radical return of the repressed which confronts them as frantic disintegration:

> I must borrow every changing shape
> To find expression . . . dance, dance
> Like a dancing bear,
> Cry like a parrot, chatter like an ape.
> (*CP*, p. 22)

In this series of phantasy metamorphoses 'self-possession' is splintered into a multitude of partial and mobile selves, just as the structuring binary oppositions of the social ego – human/non-human – collapse. The narrator's command of style miserably disintegrates. Previously the pressure of the repressed had entered the text as 'the insistent out-of-tune / Of a broken violin on an August afternoon' (*CP*, p. 20), an image whose flamboyant virtuosity assures the virtual obliteration of its alarming signified in ways familiar from 'Hysteria'. The Jamesian subtlety of the narrator's language now gives way to the non-signifying babble that is animals' cries and chattering, a breakdown of linguistic order that parallels on a larger scale the lady's own falterings. Moreover, this passage, attaining 'its effects by something not unlike caricature', represents the trace of its Marlovian 'subtext' disfiguringly scored across the poem's otherwise decorous surface.

It is fitting that immediately before this breakdown, as the speaker's self-possession gutters, he should conceive of himself as

> one who smiles, and turning shall remark
> Suddenly, his expression in a glass.
> (*CP*, p. 21)

If the mother had been unresponsive to the infant's gaze, Winnicott argued, the baby 'will grow up puzzled about mirrors and what the mirror has to offer. If the mother's face is unresponsive, then a mirror is a thing to be looked at but not to be looked into' (*PR*, p. 132). This distinction between looking at and looking into is, of course, implicit in the spectatorial distancing of the 'Portrait' of the poem's title. Mirrors are not as obligingly inert as portraits, however, and may as readily subvert as bolster the unitary ego. They may 'serve as a metaphor for the inaccessibility of one's possible selves to one's present consciousness . . . a spatial representation of an intuition that our being can never be adequately enclosed within any present formulation – any formulation here and now – of our being'.[28] Emblematic of the scandalous fact that the subject is never fully present to him or herself, the mirror may reflect back the *Doppelgänger*, the shadowy presence that haunts the subject's every least gesture and whose repression is the very condition of possibility of the stable ego. In 'Portrait of a Lady' the mirror serves a closely related fantasy function. As in *Alice through the Looking Glass*, it is an aperture giving on to a bizarre world of metamorphosis and non-signification; the narrator may not literally step through the mirror, but it is precisely this traumatic specular encounter that conjures up the frenetic parade of dancing bears, parrots and chattering apes. Ironically, then, it is not the lady's but her protégé's buried life that is alarmingly recalled, with an overwhelming power that can no longer be contained by the banal rituals of taking the air and admiring the monuments.

Should the young man ever take up psychoanalysis he will no doubt be a hardline Kleinian, committed to the centrality of the depressive position to the point where he can conceive of Winnicott's potential space only as psychotic regression, as a lunatic primitivism, a plunge into the carnivalesque madness of bears, parrots and apes. For Prufrock, by contrast, racked as he is by the psychic extremism of the paranoid–schizoid, the potential space is conceived as an easeful dissolving into infantile slumbers. Despite these differences, both poems are structured around the informing metaphor of the Raskolnikovian staircase, though I have as yet said little of the narrator's destructiveness towards the lady in 'Portrait'. A poisoned convent, Juliet's tomb, the cannibalistic tom-tom: these are pointers to the text's *coup de grâce*:

> Well! and what if she should die some afternoon,
> Afternoon grey and smoky, evening yellow and rose;
> Should die and leave me sitting pen in hand . . . .
>
> (*CP*, p. 22)

This is, first of all, one more instance of the recurrent conjunction in Eliot of an evening skyscape and a torn or dead human body. But the relation of that death to the act of writing remains uncertain, and the uncertainty is reproduced in the narrative ambiguity at this point: the narrator is either abroad in some Parisian garret writing the promised letters or, alternatively, still in London and composing the poem itself. In the first case, the act of writing is only contingently related to the lady's death – mere lost labour since its object is no longer there to receive it. In the second case, more radical possibilities open; death and writing are now more intimately interinvolved, for the former becomes the *telos* towards which all the formal strategies of the latter are deployed. It is not just that the object has disappeared, but, more eerily, that writing actively *abolishes* that object. What, the narrator ponders, if she 'should die and leave me sitting pen in hand'; but the text also suggests that this line is reversible: what if I should sit pen in hand and leave her dead?

So it is at the end of the poem that Juliet's tomb is at last filled; the four wax candles pale away into the lustre of a sunset yellow and rose, and the lady is effectively dead, her body laid out against the sky. It is only after this surge of destructive omnipotence that the young man can contemplate the specifically ethical issues thrown up by his unresponsiveness to the lady as the poem, after its fraught psychoanalytical drama, seeks to recast itself in the moral terms in which it has so often been read. But the drop in emotional pressure is obvious, and this is no self-lacerating examination:

> Not knowing what to feel or if I understand
> Or whether wise or foolish, tardy or too soon . . .
>
> (*CP*, p. 22)

In their measured complacency the antitheses merely toy with alternatives that are both beside the point. Jamesian sophistication has once more asserted itself and the text has not collapsed, as it threatened to do, into the 'savage comic humour' that menaced it; and the moment of that reassertion is the moment of the lady's death. Like Marlowe's Barabas, the poem concedes the minor charge of unfeelingness because it has already got clean away with its destructive *tour de force*.

Having opened this chapter with the riotous laughter of 'Hysteria', it seems appropriate to conclude it with the lachrymose heroine of 'La Figlia Che Piange', for that poem is also the luminous conclusion of *Prufrock and Other Observations*. 'Maiden, by what name shall I know you?' asks the epigraph, declaring the work's continuity with the themes I have traced in its predecessors. If woman in Eliot is in one aspect all that resists language, if she is nameless because she threatens a psychotic collapse that will reduce language to the non-signifying babble of apes and parrots, then the poetry itself will be the process of resisting that resistance, of conferring a name. Eliot's poems are accordingly not passive 'expressions' or 'reflections' of psychoanalytic phantasies, but rather *strategies* whereby the adult ego struggles to establish an effective distance over against the psychic conflicts that buffet it. Something of that dialectical relationship between phantasy and ego, reflection and strategy, is given in the very structure of the verbs which govern the opening lines of 'La Figlia':

Stand on the highest pavement of the stair –
Lean on a garden urn –
Weave, weave the sunlight in your hair . . . .
                                            (*CP*, p. 36)

Ambivalently situated between imperative and indicative, these
verbs at once neutrally report and actively dispose the gestures in
question. This ambiguity is in its turn reproduced in what is a
central line in a Kleinian interpretation of this poem: the girl's lover
would have left 'As the soul leaves the body torn and bruised'.
'. . . leaves' hovers undecidably between a straightforward sense of
'departure' – the soul leaves the torn and bruised body – and a
much more sinister implication of agency: the soul *renders* the body
torn and bruised. In both cases the brutality of the epithets here is a
striking dissonance; they refuse the merely illustrative role the
simile would grant them and insist on the felt presence here of a
significant phantasy. For 'La Figlia', like so many poems in this
volume, is governed by the Raskolnikovian staircase and is in quest
of 'Some way incomparably light and deft' whereby its destructive
impulse towards the woman can be at once gratified and evaded.
    This end is achieved by the textual splitting that makes the poet
simultaneously contemplative observer and dangerous participant in
the dramatised situation, a split at the level of structure that gathers
up and governs the local ambiguities I noted above. This splitting of
the ego is the obverse of a single-minded idealisation of the
woman. In so far as an aggressive sexuality does enter the poem it
takes the form not of the familiar phallic woman, but of the muted
sexual exploitativeness of the poet–lover deserting 'the body [he]
has used'. La Figlia has been aptly compared to the veiled sister of
Ash-Wednesday, for these processes of splitting and idealisation are
ones that Eliot will rely on extensively in his religious verse, and
their success is a condition of the Dantesque radiance the later
poetry strives towards. In view of these later developments it is
interesting that 'La Figlia' itself has to concede how little satisfying
these strategies are. So intense is the idealisation of the object that
the text itself laments the dissolution of psychic reality into the
sweetness of manic denial. It has sacrificed the full imagination of
'how they should have been together' with all its Dostoyevskyan
consequences for the sake of a mere 'gesture and . . . pose', and,
however light and deft the latter may be, its knowledge of evaded
aggression remains to haunt 'The troubled midnight and the

noon's repose'. These two phrases are in themselves something of a résumé of the entire volume: the former points to the unfettered paranoid–schizoid phantasies of 'Rhapsody on a Windy Night', while the latter indicates the apparently more sober depressive mode of 'Portrait of a Lady'. The repose of noon is thus rather more troubled than 'La Figlia' would care to admit, shadowed as it always is by the psychic destructiveness that is its dark underside or subtext. This poem is more successful than most in repressing that subtext, to the point where it has been read as a celebration of 'love in the lyrical sense, with no irony in the tone or context'.[29] If Eliot's texts are all strategies concerned both to do girls in and to deny the doing, then this comment by F. R. Leavis reveals that strategic sense successfully deployed on a wider scale to effect a denial of violence over the volume as a whole. Yet at the centre of 'La Figlia', as of *Prufrock and Other Observations*, stands the stark reminder of all that Eliot's lyricism would deny: 'the body torn and bruised'.

3 Carving: Hulme, Pound, Stokes and Sweeney

Ezra Pound was Eliot's first literary contact after his arrival in England in August 1914, and may well have been decisive in prompting Eliot away from the academic career he was contemplating during his dreary residence at Oxford and towards close involvement with the artistic *avant-garde* in London. The story of Pound's tireless propagandising on behalf of Eliot's work is well known, but his benevolence veered alarmingly close to a domineering patronage. While under the older poet's tutelage, Eliot suppressed his own religious poetry and embarked on the series of Sweeney poems in which violence against women eventually achieves maximum explicitness, and that violence is continuous with his early letters to Pound, littered as they are with bitterly anti-feminist remarks. Pound adumbrated his own Winnicottian diagnosis of this element in himself and Eliot when he remarked that they both suffered a 'blood poison' from America; Eliot had the disease 'perhaps worse than I have – poor devil – the thin milk of . . . New England from the pap'.[1] His involvement with Pound, T. E. Hulme and Wyndham Lewis during the years of Vorticism points to Eliot's penchant for a cult of *machismo*, which entails a rejection of paranoid–schizoid affects, a virulent anti-feminism and an authoritarian politics that ultimately found its embodiment, at least for Pound, in Benito Mussolini.

But from mid 1916 Eliot's literary horizons were expanding. Introduced by Bertrand Russell to Clive Bell, he became acquainted through Bell with the entire Bloomsbury set. Pound was well aware of the dangers of his protégé's new allegiances: 'once, when Eliot struck up an acquaintance with Roger Fry and Lowes Dickinson at the seaside in 1916, Pound behaved rather jealously, and got Eliot to agree that Fry was an ass' (*EEY*, p. 68). This confrontation between Pound and Fry, with Eliot in a no-man's-land facing crossfire from both directions, is an emblematic

58

moment. Gordan's brief account fails to make clear that this was no mere display of pettishness on Pound's part, but rather a consequence of the fundamental antagonisms between Imagism–Vorticism and Bloomsbury–Omega, whose intricate politics Richard Cork has so brilliantly charted in his *Vorticism and Abstract Art*.[2] It seems to me that this conflict can be illuminated by the psychoanalysis of Klein and Winnicott, and in this chapter I intend to concentrate on its Hulme–Pound–Lewis axis and to trace its impact on Eliot's verse. That such a juxtaposition of Klein and this group of writers is not merely fortuitous, that it is not psychoanalysis's own phantasy of theoretical omnipotence, is witnessed by the suggestive fact that between 1927 and 1929 Adrian Stokes, perhaps the most important Kleinian aesthetician, shared his enthusiasm for Italian architecture with – of all people – Ezra Pound himself.

It is with T. E. Hulme, the most articulate theorist of the poetic *avant-garde*, that a Kleinian account must begin. For Hulme, the crucial category of the literary heritage he was denouncing was *anthropomorphism*, that 'feeling of confidence in the face of the world' which characterised ancient Greece and post-Renaissance Europe and which is definitively stated by Goethe: man 'feels himself one with nature and consequently looks upon the outside world not as something strange, but as something which he recognises as answering to his own feelings' (*S*, p. 88).[3] From Hulme's viewpoint Symbolism is the last expiring gasp of this humanist heritage. The symbol may indeed effect a reciprocal recognition between subject and world, but it can do so only by fits and starts, in private chinks and crannies that inevitably risk solipsism, for the Symbolist poet has abandoned in advance vast tracts of the urban world as irredeemably other. Anthropomorphism is thus guttering out of its own accord in contemporary literature, but this is not enough for Hulme, who demands its programmatic overthrow in a return to the 'space-shyness' of Byzantine art, a relationship to the world characterised by humility, wariness and 'a certain fear' (*S*, p. 86).

Hulme's fundamental stress is this radical incompatibility of self and world: 'the necessary presupposition [of the tendency to abstraction] is the idea of a disharmony or separation between man and nature' (*S*, p. 87). This position is less fully articulated but still present in the earlier 'Romanticism and Classicism', where Hulme's stress on the accurate rendering of visual impressions by the image is a way of insisting on the distance and autonomy of both self and object which Bergsonian intuitionism would magically abolish. Poetry 'always endeavours to arrest you, and to make you continuously see a physical thing', and in the slight over-emphasis of 'continuously' a certain tension can already be detected; it is as if the object might get up to some unspecified mischief if one removed one's vigilant gaze from it for even a moment. Hulme's emphasis on the visual is thus an expression of the objectifying, mastering gaze of patriarchy which feminists such as Michèle Montrelay have denounced.[4] It could hardly be further removed from the Hegelian exchange of gazes or recognition that Winnicott saw as so fundamental a component of potential space.

So it is that for Hulme 'beauty may be in small, dry things', objects discrete and autonomous that refuse the imprint of the poet's subjectivity, whereas Romanticism tends to 'mess up, falsify and blur the clear outlines of human experience', and in its discussions of aesthetics 'always drags in the infinite' (S, p. 131). For those outlines are all that bolster the ego against the primitive merging into its environment. As Hulme obliquely recognises when he defines Romantic beauty as 'an impression of the infinite involved in the identification of our being in absolute spirit', the German Idealist aspiration towards a reconciliation of particular and universal, of finite and infinite, is only one of the pre-psychoanalytic vocabularies available for evoking the potential space. Whereas Eliot spent years involved in Bradley's neo-Hegelianism, Hulme briskly lambasted the Hegelian system in his very earliest philosophical articles; and I shall argue below that this contrast recurs in the poetic relationship of the two men.

Throughout 'Romanticism and Classicism' there runs an identification of the former term with a degenerate effeminacy, all sloppiness, moans and whining. Obscene in its rich viscous tenacity, Romanticism is 'like pouring a pot of treacle over the dinner table' (S, p. 118). This vein of imagery may be fruitfully compared with Jean-Paul Sartre's powerful evocation of *le visqueux* in *Being and Nothingness*, for the French philosopher makes inescapable the sexual significance that is only implicit in Hulme:

The slimy is *docile*. Only at the very moment when I believe that I possess it, behold by a curious reversal, *it* possesses me. Here appears its essential character: its softness is leech-like. If an object which I hold in my hands is solid, I can let go when I

please; its inertia symbolises for me my total power. . . . I open
my hands, I want to let go of the slimy and it sticks to me, it
draws at me, it sucks at me. Its mode of being is neither the
reassuring inertia of the solid nor a dynamism like that in water
which is exhausted in fleeing from me. It is a soft, yielding
action, a moist and feminine sucking, it lives obscurely under my
fingers, and I sense it like a dizziness; it draws me to it as the
bottom of a precipice might draw me.[5]

Michèle le Doeuff has convincingly demonstrated that such
nightmarish phantasies of female sexuality form the governing
metaphors of Sartre's entire epistemology in *Being and Nothingness*,[6]
and such 'moist and feminine sucking' bears an obvious relationship
to the phantasy of engulfment in the dark, rippling caverns of the
female in Eliot's 'Hysteria'. Not only does the power struggle in
the Sartrean passage cast light on Hulme's classicist formulations,
but the former's general imagery of messy physical process hints at
the latently sexual image in the latter. While the Romantic limply
surrenders himself to the supple enticements of the object, Hulme's
classicist maintains 'even in the most imaginative flights . . . a
holding back, a reservation' (*S*, p. 120). There is a subdued virile
swagger to this, evoking an icily self-possessed male haughtily
withholding his seed from a vampiric female. In the explosive
moment of Romantic *jouissance* the ego is shattered by the orgasmic
fusion of subject and object which Hulme characteristically
conceives as incorporation by the woman. By an act of imperious
self-control and withdrawal, the classical poet, 'always faithful to
the conception of a limit', will forgo that self-surrender. Hulme's
personal contempt for women, expressed by, among other ways,
his casual fornications in London tube stations, had all the
swaggering callousness of the English public-schoolboy he once
was.

That the stakes of his philosophising were always sexual was clear
to Hulme from his very first appearance in print. Discussing
Bergsonian philosophy in *The New Age*, he celebrates the intrusion
of the alogical into the certitudes of Kantianism in a flagrant image
of defloration: the philosopher Bax 'has certainly put his head
through a previously unpenetrated system, but he still remains
surrounded by the ragged edges of the medium he has destroyed'
(*FS*, p. 3). Since the long march of Hegelianism promises the
identical subject–object that the symbol delivers in an instant, it too

is associated with the woman by Hulme and subjected to a brutal
sexual manhandling by the alogical. Yet, in embracing Bergson's
doctrine that intuition may yet give an unmediated access to the
flux, Hulme was committing himself to a 'feminine' principle in
contradistinction to the conventionally patriarchal rationalism of a
Hegel. Hence there is an uneasy and self-defensive irony in his final
taunt at Bax's retreat from 'the promised land of the alogical': 'We
can only surmise maliciously that somewhere in its pleasant valleys
he saw a woman. Is not intuition too dangerous a process for an
anti-feminist to suggest as the ultimate philosophic process?' (*FS*,
p. 6).

The woman Bax saw there was perhaps the coryphée of Hulme's
'The Sunset', for such energy as Hulme's own poems still possess is
fuelled by precisely this tension between a virulent anti-feminism
and his intuitionism and its associated doctrine of the Image. 'The
Sunset', at any rate, is surely his masterpiece:

> A coryphée, covetous of applause,
> Loth to leave the stage,
> With final diablerie, poises high her toe,
> Displays scarlet lingerie of carmin'd clouds,
> Amid the hostile murmurers of the stalls.
>
> (*IP*, p. 49)

Inasmuch as the basic figure of Hulme's poetry is personification, it
might seem to contribute to that 'anthropomorphisation of the
world' (*S*, p. 54) which he so deplored. Yet he does not neglect his
own counsel to remain faithful to the conception of a limit; here,
for instance, 'coryphée' and 'diablerie', in their self-conscious
preciosity, reveal the poet's 'holding back', his refusal to commit
himself fully to his imaginative assertions. But they do rather more
than that, since it is also their function to legitimate the latent
violence of the last line. By evoking a vaguely disreputable *demi-
monde*, they conspire with the details of sexually provocative gesture
to turn the 'hostility' of the final line into the implacable wrath of a
righteous moralist. In the sexual violence that threatens, the onus of
responsibility will be placed on the self-flaunting coryphée and not
on the sinister murmurers in the stalls. '. . . diablerie' also glances
back to that literary tradition of the *femme fatale* and of deviant
sexuality that Mario Praz has charted in *Romantic Agony*, and in its
evocation of a woman at once compelling and destructive recalls

Eliot's earliest poems, which belong so decisively to that tradition. A similar dramatic situation is at issue, since the murmurers in the stalls glare as ambivalently upwards at the stage as Prufrock himself does before ascending towards his lady.

'. . . covetous of applause, / Loth to leave the stage', the coryphée exhibits all the sticky tenacity that Hulme habitually associates with the spilt treacle of Romanticism. But she not only clings, she threatens to absorb too: if the hostility is as yet only a matter of murmurs, that is surely because the audience is still rapt by her compelling performance. Her covetousness sucks her audience towards an indifferentiation of subject and object which it is the function of Hulme's Gallicisms, the faintly precious wit, to resist. They attempt to bolster a menaced identity by a narcissistic reassurance of its powers of verbal mastery in a manner reminiscent of Eliot's 'Hysteria', and their failure calls forth the hint of a more violent solution in the final line. In the adjectival insistence of 'scarlet lingerie of carmin'd clouds' is revealed another facet of the ballerina's tense fascination: she lifts her skirts only to reveal the blood-stained wound of the female's 'castration' and thereby to make horrifyingly real the possibility of the boy child's own castration. At the same time, however, her lack serves to confirm his own masculinity, reflecting back to him an image of absence which gratifyingly re-emphasises the 'fullness' of his own present possession of the phallus. Nightmarish and consoling all at once, the 'mutilated' coryphée becomes a doubly compulsive figure.

Finally, Hulme's ballerina is one of a long series of dancers whom we cannot tell from their dance which Frank Kermode in *Romantic Image* has shown to be an essential part of Symbolist iconography. While 'The Sunset' undoubtedly feels the fascination of that image, it is only to expel it all the more decisively in the menaces of its conclusion, and this brief lyric is in itself sufficient to refute Kermode's claim that Hulme offers 'a modernised, but essentially traditional, aesthetic of Symbolism'.[7] It is no accident that the icon of the dancer is so central to Symbolism. If, as I have suggested, the remote biological roots of its anthropomorphising project are indeed located in the potential space between mother and child, then the dancer too serves as testimony that the effects pertaining to the Romantic Image are related to the maternal body. Similarly, the vicissitudes the dancer undergoes in the more decadent phases of the tradition are an index of the precariousness of the recovery of potential space, of its proximity to those paranoid–schizoid terrors that play so large a role in Eliot's verse. Hulme's 'Sunset', however, refuses to succumb to the merging of self and object that its coryphée promises, and this depressive separating out from the object merits the description of pathological since it involves the implicit violence of the poem's close. This is also the case in Eliot's 'Portrait of a Lady', a text that has a close relationship to Hulme's thought, since its gushingly Romantic heroine is an emblem of the whole tradition of degenerate and loose emotionality against which Hulme fulminates in *Speculations*. Troubled by a 'dull tom-tom' and by 'hostile murmurs', both poems none the less affirm an invulnerable egoism that denies all relationship to the maternal body. This manic assertion has its historical analogy in an incident that allows me to make the transition from Hulme to Ezra Pound. In late 1913 Pound persuaded Harriet Shaw Weaver to turn over the literary pages of her feminist journal *The New Freewoman* to Imagist hands. While Weaver was still allowed to contribute feminist editorials, the success – and psychic significance – of Pound's *coup* were celebrated by the journal's brash new title: *The Egoist*.

My interest in Pound is a narrow one, confined to two aspects of his work that have been ably documented by Donald Davie in his *Ezra Pound: Poet as Sculptor*, the subtitle of which encapsulates precisely my two themes. The first is Pound's insistent use of sculptural metaphor for the poetic effects he most values. Notable instances are his definition of the Image as a 'sort of poetry where painting or sculpture seems as if it were "just coming over into speech" ' and his celebration (and exemplification) in *Hugh Selwyn Mauberley* of 'the "sculpture" of rhyme'.[8] This concern for a language that would have all the resistant materiality of marble is a figurative statement of an empiricist epistemology that believes that in the Image words and things miraculously coincide, but I intend here to tease out its psychoanalytical rather than its philosophic implications. Similarly, Pound's obsession with accuracy, with the chiselled precision of the line of verse, expresses the force of a psychic desire that Kleinian theory can illuminate as well as being a futile attempt to control the inevitable duplicities of *écriture*; and, as the case of Eliot's early work has demonstrated, signs and psyche, language and the unconscious, are not unrelated. It is Adrian Stokes himself who can mediate between Pound's sculptural analogies and the psychoanalysis of Melanie Klein, for between 1927 and 1929 the two men enjoyed a close and fertile friendship in Rapallo and

Venice. My second theme, then, is this brief convergence of their aesthetic interests and, more particularly, the light that Stokes's later, psychoanalytically oriented writings cast back on it.

As Davie has pointed out, it was their enthusiasm for the Tempio Malatestiano and the marble sculptures by Agostini di Duccio that first united Pound and Stokes. The Tempio's patron, Sigismondo Malatesta, is celebrated by Pound in Canto XVII, and Davie has claimed that Stokes's early writings, in particular his *The Stones of Rimini*, 'make an illuminating, perhaps indispensable commentary on the Cantos'. For, if the Tempio was to Stokes an outstanding example of what he termed the 'carving' tradition, it stood for Pound as the very embodiment of all the cherished values he had associated at least since *Gaudier-Brzeska* and *Mauberley* with the epithet 'cut':

> 'Cut' for him involves an admiration for cut stone, and for related arts like intaglio and the making of medals, as the image of a moral and cultural positive. In particular, he has been very interested in bas-relief; no more than Adrian Stokes could Pound agree with writers on aesthetics who see carving in low relief as a bastard form between sculpture and painting.[9]

Behind the technical interest of the Tempio stands the two writers' fascination with the impressive personality of its patron, Malatesta, whose nearest contemporary equivalent was Benito Mussolini. Stokes was eventually to distance himself from Pound over Malatesta, just as T. S. Eliot was to dissociate himself from a related figure in his 'Coriolan'. More consistent than either, Pound conflated *il Duce* with his Renaissance predecessor, and we still await a Kleinian analysis of his politics.

I wish now to turn to Adrian Stokes's account of the 'carving' tradition. In *The Quattro Cento* (1932) he identified a mode of art which had produced some of its finest manifestations in fifteenth-century Italy, but was by no means confined to that century or to any of its specific schools. In the course of attempting to distinguish this *Quattro Cento* mode from other traditions, Stokes proposes a simplified 'distinction between carving and modelling, between the use of stone and of bronze', but immediately withdraws it because 'bronze can well convey an emotion primarily imputed to the stone, while, on the other hand, stone can be carved, as it was by Lombard sculptors, to perpetuate a conception not only founded upon the model but inspired by modelling technique' (*IF*, p. 18). In *The Stones of Rimini* (1934) and *Colour and Form* (1937) Stokes refurbished this distinction, considering it now in terms not of actual physical process but rather of the artist's *attitude* towards his or her material. The defining characteristic of the carver is now love of stone as a medium, a respect for the integrity of the stone even as the artist expresses his or her phantasies through it. Far from the carver omnipotently projecting human desire onto the marble, the process is almost one of attending to expressive potentialities that are in some sense already there in the block itself; the stone itself pushes to the surface in an art of 'stone-blossom'. Associated with this regard for the autonomy of the medium is a high valuation of perspective which

> allows the externalisation of the artist's fantasy . . . in a way that does not involve any undue or assertive attack upon the stone of the kind we get with other more frankly 'illusionistic' devices for securing depth, such as undercutting or high relief. The stone remains inviolate.   (*IF*, p. 20)

In these early works the modelling tradition is ill defined and generally undervalued. Its qualities emerge by implication or by negatives and involve a merely instrumental or exploitative attitude towards the medium, a thorough subduing of it to the clamorous demands of human expressivity.

Analysed by Melanie Klein herself in the 1930s, Stokes brought his aesthetic categories into line with the Kleinian psychic positions. The fit between the carving tradition and the depressive position is clear: the carver's respect for the otherness of the medium is the depressive acknowledgement of the autonomy of the parental objects, their independence of the once-omnipotent transformations of primitive phantasy. Moreover, the work that the carver produces is itself a self-contained and coherent object, analogous both to the whole objects of the depressive position and to the coherent ego that sustains them. Technically, this self-sufficiency is achieved by the tightly knit formal structuration of the work. Bound tight by this intricate organisation, it maintains its otherness against the spectator, as in its noblest manifestations in classical Greece and the Renaissance. This classical art 'in formal impact, is obsessed with the variety and smooth interpenetration of things that in their sum symbolise an integration and independence of the self and of our objects, maybe at the expense of a blatant . . . enveloping power to which I have referred' (*IF*, p. 94).

The modelling tradition is assigned to the paranoid–schizoid position, though, as I indicated in my first chapter, that position is subdivided by Stokes into its unacceptably manic aspect and a more benign element that corresponds to Winnicott's potential space. Precariously situated along the fine line of that division, the modelled work of art has an uneasy existence in his thought. If he reinstates it in his 1955 riposte to Hanna Segal, he no less frequently deplores it, as in the above quotation, for its 'blatant . . . enveloping power'. The characteristic of the modelling tradition is its 'invitation' to the spectator, the incantatory seductions by which it dissolves the rigid boundaries of the ego and offers all the primitive delights of fusion at the breast. Formally this effect is attained by discontinuity:

> When the final balancing, the whole that is made up of interacting parts, is suspended for a time by the irregularities of stresses, these same stresses appear to gain an overwhelming, blurring, and unitary action inasmuch as the parts of the composition are thereby overrun, and inasmuch as the spectator's close participation, as if with part-objects, removes distance between him and this seeming process. (*IF*, p. 103)

The ambivalence in this process, as in Stokes's attitude to the modelled work generally, is that such dislocations are as likely to unleash the primitive terrors of the paranoid–schizoid proper as they are to achieve that beneficent fusion of self and other which is the potential space. Stokes accordingly distinguishes architecture, which obviously re-creates the enveloping maternal body, from the graphic arts, since 'graphic art as a rule insists upon the spell of inner (often persecutory) figures that stalk the mind': 'I have more concern with restoration, reparation, than with the versatile interior giants that seem to infect the artist's material with shadowy or stark power' (*IF*, pp. 68–9). We seem to be once more in that Eliotic region where the octopuses and angels wrestle.

It may then be possible to surmise that Stokes's initial over-investment in the carving tradition in *The Quattro Cento* and *The Stones of Rimini* – the very works that brought him into close association with Pound – may itself constitute a defence against the dual aspects of the paranoid–schizoid, whose affects he was only able to acknowledge adequately after his own analysis with Melanie Klein. What is sure is that the friendship between the two men loosened. As Stokes researched the background to the Tempio for a successor volume to *Stones of Rimini* he disagreed increasingly sharply with Pound's view of Sigismondo Malatesta, and his dissent here prefigures his later challenge to the one-sidedness of Hanna Segal's 'depressive' aesthetics. For Pound's insistence on Imagistic 'hardness', his relentless advocacy of precision, his desire to charge language with the dense materiality of things themselves, his recurrent sculptural metaphor, all correspond to an investment in the depressive carving-tradition that itself appears little short of pathological; and in so far as Eliot comes under Pound's influence we may expect to trace such features in his own verse, as well as a sense of their cost in terms of the psychic areas they seek to exclude.

One of the earliest measures of Eliot's rapprochement with the Hulme–Pound–Lewis axis is the curious genealogy of his 'The Death of Saint Narcissus', written in 1912, well before he had actually met Pound. Grover Smith has noted that Pound's *Ripostes* (1912) contains 'two poems influencing "The Death of Saint Narcissus"; Pound's "A Girl" and T. E. Hulme's "Conversion" '.[10] Hulme's brief lyric, like his 'The Sunset', evokes a Symbolist aesthetic only to turn brutally upon it in the poem's closing lines:

> Light-hearted I walked into the valley wood
> In the time of hyacinths,
> Till beauty like a scented cloth
> Cast over, stifled me. I was bound
> Motionless and faint of breath
> By loveliness that is her own eunuch.
>
> Now pass I to the final river
> Ignominiously, in a sack, without sound,
> As any peeping Turk to the Bosphorus.
>
> (*IP*, p. 18)

As its title intimates, 'Conversion' is a more programmatic text than 'The Sunset'. Whereas the latter felt the fascination of a Romantic merging of self and other, but still resisted it, 'Conversion' records only an inglorious capitulation. The imprisoning 'sack' of the penultimate line is an external perspective on what is experienced as a subjective enveloping in the first stanza: beauty 'stifles' with all the dense, oozing energy of Sartre's *le visqueux*, for the thick, cloying scent it exudes is only a more refined version of the 'slimy'. Occurring in the 'time of hyacinths', Hulme's epiphany invites comparison with a later moment of ecstasy in a hyacinth garden, and the watery fate of his protagonist may cast some light on the obscure events that take place there ('Your arms full, and your hair wet' – *CP*, p. 64). Ending resoundingly with 'eunuch', the stanza also suggests that its stifling absorption may be a castrating attack and this is more obliquely implied by the poem's closing line. Behind 'any peeping Turk' we can hardly fail to sense the pressure of the more familiar colloquialism 'peeping Tom': it may therefore be conjectured that the ignominious victim of 'Conversion' was one of the sinister murmurers who in 'The Sunset' peeped at the ballerina's lingerie to confront the carmin'd scandal of female 'castration'. That earlier discovery that beauty was a eunuch was, I argued, deeply ambivalent; here it is straightforwardly overwhelming.

Yet for all this the text is not merely defeated. 'Peeping Tom' is repressed into a shadowy semantic limbo, and the jingoistic brashness of the final image asserts a swaggering energy that the poem had seemed drained of, serving as a forceful reminder of Hulme's allegiance with the militaristic–imperialist poets of the Edwardian years and discomfortingly suggesting the political implications of his classicism. By a deft sleight of hand, the image displaces onto the Turks the violence the poem itself had seemed victim of, and it therefore ends as it began, 'light-hearted'. In the tossing of the protagonist into the river there may even be an allusion to primitive fertility rituals whereby the text slyly grants itself the promise of a rebirth;[11] a Romantic fusion of self and other may have carried the day, but the classicist will regroup his forces to begin the fight anew.

And the fight is indeed carried on in Pound's 'A Girl', which alludes to the myth of Daphne, turned into a bay-tree at her own request to escape the pursuit of Apollo:

> The tree has entered my hands,
> The sap has ascended my arms,
> The tree has grown into my breast . . . .
> *(SP*, p. 14)

It is illuminating to juxtapose these lines with Leo Bersani's account of Baudelairean sadism in his *Baudelaire and Freud*:

> Baudelaire's misogyny can be understood partly in terms of a panicky effort to reject the feminine side of his own sexual nature, and, more generally, to put an end to the psychic scattering or self-dissemination of desire. [His] sadism is an attempt to stop the woman from moving, for her movements excite desires which may both endanger her and reduce the poet's identity to a kind of mobile fragmentariness. The loved one's stillness is a crucial sign of a major Baudelairean enterprise: that of immobilizing desire.[12]

If we recast this in Winnicottian terms, arguing that the woman's movements evoke the possibility of that 'mobile fragmentariness' that potential space necessarily appears to be from the depressive perspective, then it is clear that Pound values the Daphne myth as just such a phantasy of female immobility. The myth even presents such immobilising as the woman's own desire and thereby evades that risk of the return of sadism upon the self by the persecutory superego which haunts Baudelaire's verse. None the less, it is only a tamer form of a project whose logical extreme Bersani describes as 'necrophilia . . . the Baudelairean erotic ideal; it is sex with an absolutely still partner who, at the extreme, may even be devoured'.[13] Not quite necrophiliac, Pound's distasteful little poem nevertheless records a murderously thorough sexual penetration, contriving to satisfy its Apollo even at the moment when, traditionally, his violent desire was definitively frustrated.

So convenient did Pound find this myth that he used it again in *Hugh Selwyn Mauberley*, at a time when his association with Eliot was particularly close:

> 'Daphne with her thighs in bark
> Stretches toward me her leafy hands,' –
> Subjectively. In the stuffed-satin drawing-room
> I await The Lady Valentine's commands.
>
> (*SP*, p. 180)

The Lady Valentine is another version of the society hostess so ambivalently celebrated in Eliot's 'Portrait of a Lady'. Like Hulme's Romantic poet, she blurs and smears all the wiry outlines to which the classicist tenaciously clings, and Pound's satire touches deep fears of that enveloping absorption of the self which Hulme treated in 'Conversion':

> Poetry, her border of ideas,
> The edge, uncertain, but a means of blending
> With other strata
> Where the lower and higher have ending.
>
> (*SP*, p. 180)

Assured of certain certainties about where self and world begin and end, the carver can only experience such dubious edges and blendings as a murky and irresistible vortex that threatens to suck in and splinter his punctilious self-possession. Small wonder, then, that the poem must begin with a phantasy of the woman's deathly immobilisation before it can achieve the self-assurance and poise necessary to its satiric purpose. In its Poundian inflection the Daphne myth is a phantasy of male mastery, and it therefore relieves the smouldering social resentment of a lowly *littérateur* humiliatingly at the Lady Valentine's command. At the same time, however, the Daphne lines display a lyricism that is foreign to the rest of the text, with its clipped rhythms and its Jamesian use of uncomfortably placed and dislocating interjections. Stretching out her leafy hands, Daphne is offering an 'invitation' like that Adrian Stokes considered characteristic of the modelled art work, and it is in reaction to this that the syntax of the subsequent stanzas closes ranks, rigidly marshalling four and a half verses within the span of a single sentence. With all the ambiguity of a compromise formation, the myth thus has a numinosity that leaves the depressive aplomb of the rest of the poem looking distinctly mean and pinched, even as it satisfies the phantasy violence that made that cool self-possession possible in the first place. Hinting at the *cost* as well as blazoning the success of this pathological version of the depressive position, Pound's poem points to the more radical ambivalences that the associated texts of Eliot will show.

While Eliot's 'The Death of Saint Narcissus' (*PEY*, pp. 34–5) is located within the general ambit of 'Conversion' and 'A Girl', it operates a profound subversion of its parent texts. Announcing itself as a cautionary exemplum – 'I will show you his bloody cloth and limbs' – it is every bit as doctrinaire as Hulme's 'Conversion', but its antagonistic relationship to its predecessors is first evident *formally.* Whereas Pound and Hulme's lyrics are taut and cohesive, achieving a formal integration that closes them upon themselves, 'Saint Narcissus' is best described by its own epithet 'sprawling'. The Imagistic hardness of 'Conversion' and 'A Girl' rebuffs the empathy of the Romantic reader, while Eliot's poem invites its readership to a 'surrender' that its protagonist will achieve only in death. For Saint Narcissus is almost a parody of classicist self-possession: far from being menaced with absorption by his world, he is locked in a solipsistic enclosure, 'stifled and soothed by his own rhythm'. Rigidly refusing the seductions of the spring landscape, he rises to a bizarre pitch of self-consciousness:

> His eyes were aware of the pointed corners of his eyes
> And his hands were aware of the pointed tips of his fingers.
>
> (*PEY*, p. 34)

There could be no finer *reductio ad absurdum* of the coolly self-assured narrator of 'Portrait of a Lady'. But the cost of this strenuous maintenance of identity is the string of phantasy identifications – tree, fish and girl – that constitutes the central section of the poem and which parallels the carnivalesque bears, parrots and apes of the 'Portrait'; once again the ego is psychotically dispersed in a Baudelairean 'mobile fragmentariness'. Whereas the tree image in Pound was a device of immobilisation, the tree in 'Saint Narcissus' is frenetically 'twisting' and 'tangling' in an effort to achieve the merging of self and world that the classicist aims to deny. Similarly, the writhing 'slippery white belly' of the fish is a vivid tactile evocation of Sartrean sliminess; it is an index of repressed areas of subjectivity 'held tight' by the fingers of an imperious will. But the will falters to the point where the brutal rape of the third phantasy is the only means of quelling a 'young girl' who we may take to be a Symbolist dancer. 'Saint Narcissus' thus makes explicit the sexual violence of its predecessors, but does so with a notable change of tone: whereas the Turks and Daphne were disposed of with considerable relish, here the rape is unrelievedly sordid, its perpetrator 'drunken and old'.

'So he became a dancer to God.' By compacting its Narcissus with Saint Sebastian the poem finds a way out of its solipsism. The environment now attacks the self with an energy far beyond the mere 'stifling' of Hulme's 'Conversion', but this invasion is masochistically welcomed:

Because his flesh was in love with the burning arrows
He danced on the hot sand
Until the arrows came.
As he embraced them his white skin surrendered itself to the
   redness of blood, and satisfied him.

(PEY, p. 35)

The rape of the third phantasy now bounces back in persecutory
form upon the subject, and the poem by the same token reverses the
sexual immobilisation of Pound's 'A Girl', permitting a 'surrender'
of self to environment that it was precisely the theoretical purpose
of Hulme's stress on *dis*continuity to outlaw. Nor is this really
surprising in the author of *Knowledge and Experience in the Philosophy
of F. H. Bradley*. For both Bradley and Eliot the ego, whose
autonomy Pound and Hulme are at all costs concerned to defend, is
not fundamental, is indeed no more than an arbitrary construction
upon the welter of immediate experience; and there could
accordingly be no more theoretically wrong-headed procedure than
investing it with the status of ultimate reality, however
experientially desirable that may have seemed to Eliot at times.
'Saint Narcissus' closes with 'the shadow in his mouth' and this is
its oblique testimony that the distant source of the psychotic drama
it plays out is a breakdown in the oral relationship to the maternal
breast. Eliot has drawn on Hulme and Pound only to subvert them,
to reveal the psychic cost of their rejection of areas of subjectivity
that they identify as 'female' in the name of their cult of tight-
lipped *machismo*. Unlike Hulme and Wyndham Lewis, Eliot did not
attend an English public school, an undoubted boon in these
matters.

   The transition between *Prufrock and Other Observations* and *Poems
1920* is decisively made in 'The Love Song of Saint Sebastian',
whose title suggests the close relationship Eliot felt it bore to his
earlier and more celebrated Love Song. 'Saint Sebastian' was
written in 1914:

In the first fantasy the lover flogs himself at the foot of the lady's
stair until his blood flies. She is there watching in a white gown.
His martyrdom attracts her attention and, in pity, she calls him
to her bed where he dies between her breasts. In the second
fantasy the lover's relation to the lady is reversed. This time he is
a sexual menace, exerting brute power over the white-clad body

he loves. He comes at her with a towel and bends her head beneath his knees, fingering the curve of her ear. When he strangles her . . . she loves him more.   (*EEY*, p. 28)

I shall discuss the first part of this poem in connection with Eliot's religious verse, which it clearly anticipates. In the second phantasy there is an accession of psychic confidence. No longer does the destructiveness have to be denied in relation to the woman by being displaced onto the speaker's self: more than acknowledged, it is now voluptuously lingered over, though the death between the lady's breasts in the first section should alert us that it is the infant-mother, rather than a sexual, relationship that is fundamentally at issue here. Or rather Eliot's poetry is now entering an extended depressive phase in which the relation to the object is characterised by genital rather than pre-genital impulses. So it is that Prufrock's desire to 'bite off the matter with a smile' will give way to the brash genitality declared by the title 'Sweeney Erect'.

Saint Sebastian's second love-song alludes to Robert Browning's 'Porphyria's Lover', in which a remarkably lucid lunatic voluptuously throttles his mistress with the tresses of her own hair in order to preserve intact the moment of her perfect acquiescence to him. And behind that poem we sense the presence of Browning's 'My Last Duchess'. There the tormenting because living Duchess is transformed by an act of violence so elided as to be almost beyond the poem's ken ('I gave commands; / Then all smiles stopped together') into the delicate portrait which graces the Duke's gallery, a perfect sign that defers even as it delivers presence, resembling in that respect the ambivalent staircase of Eliot's early verse and the preserved corpse of the mistress in *Sweeney Agonistes*. More relevant still to Eliot is the status of 'My Last Duchess' in the Browning canon. As one of the first of Browning's dramatic monologues, it represents his abandonment of the early Romantic-confessional manner of *Pauline* and *Paracelsus* in the name of a 'classicism' guaranteed by the impersonality of the monologue: 'so many utterances of so many imaginary persons, not mine'.[14] The poem does not simply record that transition, it *enacts* it, and in terms peculiarly relevant to Kleinian and Winnicottian psychoanalysis. What so stings the Duke about his Duchess is her instant receptivity to her environment, for she is a veritable paragon of Keatsian negative capability, 'A heart . . . Too easily impressed'. Exceeding the mark that the Duke affirms as inviolate boundary between self and other, her responsiveness is tantamount to a complete dispersal of the ego into potential space and is imaged by the Duke as the obscene openness, the immediate availability, of the whore; such at least seems to be the underlying identification in his clipped comment that 'her looks went everywhere'. The Duke, by contrast, is depressive to a fault, solipsistic in his refusal of relationship: 'I choose / Never to stoop'. The brutal violence that hovers just off the page is, then, the revenge of a pathologically depressive character on the 'feminine' side of its own nature. Such violence need not undergo the more radical transformations that mark its appearance in Eliot's Sweeney poems, because the very social situation of Browning's text allows its easy displacement beyond the elegant aestheticism of aristocratic life; as for killing our wives, our servants will do that for us. Winnicott's work suggests that any post-Romantic 'return' to classicism will involve this negation of the potential space as the psychic territory in which Romantic poetry itself so often operates; and the cost of this negation will be the unleashing of the paranoid–schizoid fears and strategies with which Klein has familiarised us. If this cursory attention to Browning prompts this hypothesis, prolonged study of T. S. Eliot abundantly confirms it.

A poem which mediates by a rather different route between *Prufrock and Other Observations* and *Poems 1920* is 'Mr Apollinax', a text which celebrates Eliot's acquaintance with Bertrand Russell. Insisting on the independence of the object of experience from the subject's experience of it, Russell might be termed the philosopher of the depressive position, and he and G. E. Moore were leading rebels in the early years of the century against the idealism of Eliot's mentor Bradley. The 'new realism' of Russell and Moore swiftly gained ground in the Harvard philosophy department, and Russell was visiting professor there while Eliot was a graduate. Involved in the intricacies of neo-Hegelianism, the young poet had no time for Russell's realism and its yoking of philosophy to mathematics, but he struck up an allegiance with the English philosopher against the aridities of New England protocol. 'Mr Apollinax' is strategically situated in the *Collected Poems* just after such desiccated sketches of Boston life as 'The *Boston Evening Transcript*' and 'Aunt Helen', and the poet's alliance with Apollinax against New England's 'army of unalterable law' is expressed in the latter's brazen phallic energy, which halts just this side of unleashed violence:

I heard the beat of centaur's hoofs over the hard turf
As his dry and passionate talk devoured the afternoon.

(*CP*, p. 33)

That turf resists the hoof in a way that the paranoid–schizoid world of 'Prufrock' did not; it refuses the imprint of subjectivity. Similarly, the dry passion of Apollinax's talk contrasts with the enervating musical cadences of 'Prufrock', its voices dying with a dying fall. Subject and object are as discrete as Russell and Moore themselves could have wished, and this depressive world is governed by an insistent genital sexuality – Priapus, the centaur – which was also celebrated by the Vorticist Gaudier-Brzeska in his carving of 'Ezra in the form of a marble phallus'.

Formally very different from 'Prufrock', 'Mr Apollinax' none the less consistently refers back to that earlier poem; its academic milieu of tinkling afternoon teacups is another version of the drearily refined social rituals Prufrock contemplates. It is as if impulses which were scattered and ineffectual in 'Prufrock' were lifted wholesale out of that text, hitched to the formidable phallic energy of Mr Apollinax, and thereby enabled to sweep to a psychic victory that had previously seemed far beyond them. Prufrock's pre-genitality is not abolished but refurbished by the phallic prowess of his successor: the former may have failed to bite off the matter with a smile, but the latter triumphantly 'devours' the afternoon, and his hapless victims, Mrs Phlaccus and Professor and Mrs Cheetah, are metamorphosed into 'a slice of lemon, and a bitten macaroon'. The power relations evoked in 'Prufrock' are both recalled and reversed; the lady's dismissive 'That is not what I meant at all' now becomes the feeble and wistful reflection that 'There was something he said that I might have challenged' (*CP*, pp. 16, 33). Even the hint of a Saloméan decapitation somehow loses its menace. Whereas Prufrock's head 'brought in upon a platter' is merely an inert exhibit, 'the head of Mr Apollinax rolling under a chair' seems only another facet of the man's bizarre and all-pervasive vitality (*CP*, pp. 16, 33). Far from being quelled, Apollinax carries off this hint of castration with an even greater swagger. 'Prufrock' thus lurks behind the virile façade of 'Mr Apollinax' as its parasitic subtext, with something of the manner of the young T. S. Eliot attaching himself to more flamboyant and aggressive males such as Russell and Ezra Pound.[15]

But the poem also reserves a corner for other Prufrockian

emotions; while Priapus gapes at the lady in the swing, the narrator
thinks 'of Fragilion, that shy figure among the birch-trees'.
Fragilion is the trace in 'Mr Apollinax' of the various evocations of
the potential space in its predecessor poem – the fog curled round
the house, the evening stretched somnolently on the floor – and in
the central phantasy corresponding to this presence the familiar
enervated rhythms recur:

> His laughter was submarine and profound
> Like the old man of the sea's
> Hidden under coral islands
> Where worried bodies of drowned men drift down in the green
>   silence,
> Dropping from fingers of surf.
>   (*CP*, p. 33)

The staple style of the poem, its taut two or three-line syntactical
units, momentarily falters. Unlike the image of the 'irresponsible
foetus', the simile of the old man of the sea refuses its punctual
satiric point, generating instead a submarine depth of its own. This
is not the 'hard turf' of line 16, but rather a Stokesian 'invitation'.
The sentence itself 'drifts down' as its syntax meanders forward,
not so much halting at the full stop as seeping across into the
meditative white space that separates the two verse paragraphs of
the poem; and so lulling is this phantasy that it will take something
of a lurch to get the text underway again. If, earlier, 'Cheetah's'–
'foetus' was a brashly depressive rhyme, the more subtle 'islands'–
'silence' might perhaps be dubbed a Winnicottian one. '. . .
worried' is interestingly ambiguous. The bodies are doubtless
worried in the sense that Phlebas's will be in *The Waste Land*,
subject to the slow oral attacks of underwater creatures, yet little of
the paranoid terror that that prospect can provoke in Eliot is
allowed to impinge here. Still in touch with 'irresponsible' four
lines earlier, 'worried' may also have a sufficient moral weight to
evoke a depressive superego whose judgement on Apollinax's
destructiveness – 'He laughed like an irresponsible foetus' – is
rather more robust than Fragilion's shy retiring behind the birch-
trees. The underwater phantasy that was the merest escapism at the
end of 'Prufrock' has here become a source of psychic growth. The
poem thereby announces that the potential space, far from being
regressive, is necessary if the reparative impulses of the depressive

position are to be fully mobilised. 'Mr Apollinax' judges, even as it celebrates and exploits to its own ends, a figure 'so firmly anchored in objectively perceived reality that [he is] ill in the opposite sense of being out of touch with the subjective world and with the creative approach to fact' (*PR*, p. 78). That figure will dominate *Poems 1920* in the form of Sweeney, for the volume dramatises a depressive separating out from the object in which reparative impulses are minimal, which is indeed rather the occasion for a new frankness of aggression against the female body.

Poems 1920 contains work written during the year of Eliot's closest association with Pound:

> two authors, neither engaged in picking the other's pocket, decided that the dilutation of *vers libre* . . . had gone too far and that some countercurrent must be set going. . . . Remedy prescribed *Emaux et Camées*. Rhyme and regular strophes. Results: Poems in Mr Eliot's second volume . . . also H. S. Mauberley.[16]

Vers libre was from the start the weak point of the Imagist programme. In one aspect it may have been conducive to a poetic of 'hardness', since it allowed the poem to be disciplined by the very textures of the object to be presented. But it was no less likely to license the rhythmic effusions of Amy Lowell's Polyphonic Prose, which, in its impressionistic notation of the moment-by-moment interchange of self and world, has close affinities with such Bloomsbury products as *Mrs Dalloway* and *To the Lighthouse*. From this viewpoint Pound and Eliot's crusade against free verse is a logical conclusion of their deciding that Roger Fry was an ass.

The psychic consequences of their espousal of Gautier were drastic, as is evidenced by Eliot's praise of the poetry of Jean de Bosschère for 'an intense frigidity which I find altogether admirable'.[17] Its formal consequences were little less so. There is a systematic purging of the incantatory rhythms and discontinuities of 'Prufrock' in favour of tightly articulated quatrains which aspire not to the condition of music, but rather to Pound's ' "sculpture " of rhyme'. Yet these are not quite poems in the carving tradition as celebrated by Adrian Stokes, for even as the carver imposes a phantasy on the stone he or she attends and responds to the artistic structures suggested by the material itself: 'he elicits meaning from a substance, precious for itself, whose subsequent forms made by the chisel were felt to be pre-existent and potential' (*IF*, p. 99). In the quatrain poems, however, Eliot submits his language to pre-given limits of association; hence the familiar complaint that these verses have all the brittle cleverness of the acrostic. Stokes's stress on the interplay between carver and medium suggests that this relationship has the characteristics of Winnicott's potential space. Even in the depressive artefact, insisting on its autonomy, there has occurred in the making of it an indifferentiation of subject and object such that it is unclear whether the artefact is creation or discovery; the carver has, paradoxically, imposed an order that was somehow always already given. It would seem, then, as Eliot's own 'Mr Apollinax' had hinted, that the potential space remains an essential constituent of a full access to the depressive position. Its denial, and it is indeed denied in Eliot's summary manipulations of his linguistic medium, results in a separating out from the object that is no more than a mode of manic defence.

This dominative relationship to the sign may be explored a little further, for it characterises the very project of an Imagist poetic. In theory the Imagist lyric holds itself sensitively open to receive the exact impress of its object, but in practice this goal of fidelity involves a tireless manipulating of the medium, the strenuous bending of language to the very contours of its object, a severe policing of the text to ensure that no word goes wasted or astray. In Hulme the act of writing entails a violent expenditure of muscular tension in the effort to subdue a recalcitrant medium. The poet does not work with architect's curves but with 'a springy piece of steel':

> the state of tension or concentration of mind, if he is doing anything really good in this struggle against the ingrained habit of the technique, may be represented by a man employing all his fingers to bend the steel out of its own curve and into the exact curve which you want. (*S*, p. 133)

This compositional *agon* is also in contradiction with Imagism's Bergsonian epistemology, for which the poem is an end in itself, a Schopenhauerian withdrawing from the contingencies of action that affords a pure and contemplative glimpse of things as they are in themselves. Rejecting a linguistic utilitarianism that would yoke the lyric to extraneous ends, rhetorical or moralistic, Imagism none the less finds itself reaffirming such instrumentalism at the level of *texture*: every word must be ruthlessly functional, ordered in a strict regime that is a triumph of linguistic administration: 'When the analogy has not enough connection with the thing described to be quite parallel with it, where it overlays the thing it described and there is a certain excess, there you have the play of fancy – that I grant is inferior' (*S*, p. 138). It is this 'excess', the bewildering play of signs above and beyond their representational function, that all this frenetic insistence on precision aims at mastering.

Hulme's desire to exert the maximum possible control over meaning is shared by Ezra Pound, who advised the poetic aspirant to 'consider the way of the scientist rather than the way of an advertising agent for a new soap' (*IP*, p 132). In this empiricist myth of the scientist Pound extols a patient but unswerving matching of words to things in one-to-one correspondences against the superficial patter of the commercial, but his image has a Hulmean 'excess' of its own that disturbs this clear-cut comparison. It is the *product* advertised more than the institution of advertising that is relevant here, for the relationship of soap to body is curiously like that of the Imagist lyric to its object, and in each case is an instance of what Jacques Derrida has termed the 'logic of supplementarity'. Soap is apparently extraneous to a human body that is, by nature, complete in itself, and yet at the same time it completes the body, as culture does Nature, rendering it more itself than it would otherwise have been, which is the very service the Image performs for its object. Yet this relationship is not simply beneficial. Soap does not courteously efface itself before the full presence of the restored body, but rather possesses an alarming principle of proliferation which in its rich abundance of froth, suds and lather threatens to engulf the merely natural, just as the Image, by its semantic duplicities or 'excess', threatens to eclipse rather than body forth its object. Pound's own image thus subversively suggests that advertising prattle menaces the laconic scientist from within, that no amount of precision and paring will succeed in stilling the dance of signs. However abrasively the Imagist scrubs away at his medium in an effort to conform it to the object, all he will generate is 'the Shallow frothy excitement of writing' (*IP*, p. 141).

If the classicist ego cannot tolerate the unstable, contradictory 'boundaries' of Winnicott's potential space, no more can it brook the mercurial and slippery movements of *écriture*, for both jeopardise its own transcendental status. Since, as recent feminists have argued, it is characteristically women who tend to live a diffuse, bodily relationship to script under patriarchy, the classicist's violence against the elusive sign is always latently violence against the woman; to immobilise the latter is at the same time to contain the former's 'excess'. But even in Eliot's quatrain poems the sign is not easily quelled: straitened within the taut syntax of the body of the text, it explodes all the more excessively in the bewildering pyrotechnics of the epigraph to 'Burbank with a Baedeker: Bleistein with a Cigar' (*CP*, pp. 42–3).

Within this chaos familiar motifs stand out. A Latin inscription from Mantegna's painting of Saint Sebastian points a connection with the reciprocal violences of Eliot's second Love Song. The compacting of allusions to Browning and *Othello* evokes the persecutory bad object: from the former comes a phantasy of the annihilated object – 'dear dead women, with such hair too' ('A Toccata of Galuppi's') – which is then charged with all the sexual voracity conveyed in Othello's brutal interjection 'Goats and monkeys!' (*Othello*, Act IV, scene i). The epigraph's final lines are the stage directions at the close of Marston's *Entertainement of Alice, Dowager Countess*. Though initially puzzling in their lack of Venetian connotation, they now take their psychic place as the evocation of an idealised mother figure, Niobe, who is needed to cope with the dangerous presence of her sexualised counterpart.

Burbank's Baedeker aligns him with the traditional values of Renaissance Venice which have fallen into squalid contemporary decline, and in the context I have outlined in this chapter we may interpret those values as that massive investment in a depressive separating out from the maternal object that Stokes found in the carving tradition of the *Quattro Cento*, and which was personified for Ezra Pound in Malatesta. But Burbank has sacrificed the very principle of his masculinity to a woman who is envisaged as herself lifeless – 'meagre, blue-nailed, phthisic' – but insatiably vampiric upon the male substance. The God Hercules leaves him, just as he was to leave Adrian Stokes in the course of the Kleinian analysis that eventually allowed him to respond to the 'invitation' of the modelling-tradition. Burbank is supplanted by Bleistein, for the Jew incarnates a phantasy of the indifferentiation of self and other nightmarishly viewed from an extreme depressive perspective:

> A lustreless protrusive eye
>   Stares from the protozoic slime
> At a perspective of Canaletto.
>   (*CP*, pp. 42–3)

Here, in brief compass, is an evocation of *le visqueux* to match Jean-Paul Sartre's own for intertwined fascination and disgustingness; as the 'saggy bending' of Bleistein's knees suggests, the very outlines of the human form are dissolved in the seepings and oozings of 'protozoic slime'. It is particularly ironic that he should stare at the limpid canal scenes of the Italian painter, for, as Sartre comments,

> Slime is the agony of water . . . there is a sticky thickness in its liquidity; it represents a dawning triumph of the solid over the liquid – that is, a tendency of the indifferent in-itself, which is represented by the pure solid, to fix the liquidity, to absorb the for-itself which ought to dissolve it.[18]

In Bradleyan terms this sliminess is a horrific vision of immediate experience, that primal indifferentiation which exists before the crystallising out into subject and object marked by the poem's stress on Canaletto's use of perspective. Even the Jew's cosmopolitanism – 'Chicago Semite Viennese' – is thrown accusingly at him as a transgression of rigidly defined national frontiers, which Eliot in a less negatively Bradleyan phase would have spurned as mere arbitrary constructions upon the shapeless welter of immediate experience. It is this dense and gooey substance, the poem surely implies, that the Lady Volupine needs to replenish her meagre veins.

While 'Burbank with a Baedeker: Bleistein with a Cigar' laments the former's seduction by the blandishments of the female, 'Whispers of Immortality' (*CP*, pp. 55–6) avoids such a fate by the line of dots that breaks the back of the poem at the end of its fourth stanza. On the far side Grishkin's uncorseted and 'friendly bust/Gives promise of pneumatic bliss', a promise that bears comparison with Stokes's 'invitation'. But, whatever else they are, busts in Eliot are never casually friendly, and, as the subsequent image of the 'couched Brazilian jaguar' reveals, the poet's breezy poise is not so easily maintained. Indeed its full cost has already been made apparent on the near side of the poem's division, where Donne and Webster engage in a concentrated production of destructive phantasies:

> And saw the skull beneath the skin;
> And breastless creatures under ground
> Leaned backward with a lipless grin.
>
> (*CP*, p. 55)

As in Pound's *Hugh Selwyn Mauberley*, XII, the woman must be stilled before she can be safely satirised. The daffodil bulbs of the next stanza hint at a reparative impulse in the seasonal terms *The Waste Land* will make much of, but here their restorative connotations are overlain by the grim finality with which they 'Stared from the sockets of the eyes'; this is a fixed and non-mirroring maternal gaze. In stanzas three and four, John Donne is recast as a version of Eliot's Hamlet: 'expert beyond experience', he has an inner vision of such power that 'no contact possible to flesh' can allay it. In 'Hamlet and his Problems' Shakespeare's protagonist is equally incapable of achieving 'complete adequacy of the external to the emotion'. Both character and play are 'full of some stuff that the writer could not drag to light' and which Eliot locates in Hamlet's relationship to his mother (*SE*, p. 144). In Kleinian terms, Eliot's Hamlet, like the John Donne of 'Whispers of Immortality', remains in the paranoid–schizoid organisation, relating not to the real objects of the external world but to the internal figures of his own phantasies. Sadistic impulses to 'seize and clutch and penetrate' inevitably rebound on the subject as the persecutory anguish, ague and fever of the fourth stanza. The taut power of these early verses is the construction of a psychic armour-plating that will license the casual witticisms that will then play around an alarming female figure notable for the abundance of her mammaries.

Yet Eliot's irony is never stable. Earlier, his Laforguian persona was never quite sure whether his performance was a languidly self-possessed display of linguistic serendipity or, on the other hand, a compulsive babbling of which his self was mere effect and not master. Similarly, he could never entirely decide whether the woman herself was a mistress of the sign, her every laconic utterance constituting an orderly regime of sense that brooked no contradiction, or whether, after all, she was merely an obtuse socialite doling out tired clichés in response to his glamorous effusions. Later, in *The Waste Land*, Eliot's cultural allusions will never quite know whether they are denouncing an impoverished present in the name of a spiritual plenitude that once existed in the historical past or whether, on the contrary, they are demonstrating a continuity of spiritual hollowness across the centuries; does the past exist on the other side of some tragic 'dissociation of sensibility' or is it merely the drab present tricked out in Elizabethan regalia? A parallel ambivalence afflicts the later verses of

'Whispers of Immortality'. The couched Brazilian jaguar with her 'subtle effluence of cat' reduces Grishkin's maisonnette to banality. Against the rich and dangerous eroticism of Nature, all Culture has to show are the practical conveniences and stage properties of modern fornication; and the semi-colon at the end of this stanza's third line holds open a space which affirms the utter distinctness of Nature and Culture even as it savours the full garish bathos of their contrast. But there is a kind of seepage of meaning across that very semi-colon: the Kleinian splitting whereby the sinister and devouring aspects of the female are sheared away from the easy sexual availability of Grishkin does not altogether hold, as is clear in the next stanza:

> The sleek Brazilian jaguar
> Does not in its arboreal gloom
> Distil so rank a feline smell
> As Grishkin in a drawing-room.

The satiric gestures of punctuation vanish as the split elements now fuse; as at moments in *The Waste Land*, continuity rather than contrast comes to the fore. More even than this: Culture actually *outdoes* Nature in what had until then seemed Nature's exclusive preserve. The 'sleekness' of the jaguar now seems to belong with the clean lines and angles of the modern maisonette (and of the sex that takes place within it), while in her 'rankness' Grishkin has expropriated Nature of its most coarse and luxuriant energies; and the epithet 'rank' carries something of the twinned fascination and loathing of Sartre's 'slimy'. So it is that in the final stanza it is no longer Grishkin who is satirised but rather 'our lot'; projected irony has returned in persecutory form upon the subject. Grishkin is no longer a mere (wo)man of straw but a compelling force that subjugates even the 'Abstract Entities' to her centripetal fascination, and reduces the apparently formidable Donne and Webster of the early verses to a feebly escapist burrowing between 'dry ribs'.

It is Sweeney who takes up the struggle against the woman dejectedly abandoned in 'Whispers of Immortality'. 'Sweeney Erect' (*CP*, pp. 44–5) obviously flaunts phallic sexuality, but in its reference to the human animal as 'erectus' also recalls Freud's speculations on humankind's adoption of the upright stance and its consequent abandonment of the sense of smell.[19] Smell in Eliot's poetry is more often than not concerned, in ways both disgusting and enticing, with the overpowering proximity of the female body. The 'perfume from a dress' delicately wafting to Prufrock's nostrils (*CP*, p. 15) is the exception rather than the rule here, for the woman's smell is usually a dense, heated animality. Princess Volupine's name, with its foxy connotations, is a hint that is developed with brutal explicitness in Grishkin's rank feline smell and in the 'good old hearty female stench' of Fresca in *The Waste Land* manuscript (where the 'heartiness' is all bluff). These connotations even afflict Eliot's 'Dedication to my Wife', with its discomforting reference to 'lovers whose bodies smell of each other' (*CP*, p. 234). Is this a courageous acknowledgement of the physicality of sex to which one's uneasy response is merely puritanical, or should it simply never have got into the poem in the first place, being only one more attempt to brazen out an old ambivalence? A voracious adult sexuality clearly underpins these references to female smells: unlike Sweeney erect, brazenly parading his arousal, the woman's sexuality is hidden, interior, folded claustrophobically away within the body like the 'female smells in shuttered rooms' of Eliot's 'Rhapsody' (*CP*, p. 28). The woman is thus not to be trusted, for she may be secreting her heated sexual juices even in the most unlikely moments; sophisticated chatter about Michelangelo is no guarantee that in its concealed depths her body is not pursuing a rank, viscous life of its own. The most striking image of this discrepancy between female intellect and corporality are the astounding lines about Fresca in the draft of *The Waste Land*, in which she reads Richardson as she s(h)its in the lavatory (*WLF*, p. 23). And that anal reference points to more primitive impulses behind the obsession with female smell, for behind the fear of women's genital sexuality are those primordial memories where bodies smelt of each other because they were not yet distinguishable into mine and hers, body-ego and the other. From this viewpoint, then, the insistence of Sweeney's upright posture declares his stern renunciation of the maternal potential space. The sensual delights of smell, which were connected in the first place to one's own faeces, must be repressed because the faeces are themselves dangerously ambivalent. Part of the body yet detachable, intimate interior products that are none the less casually disposable, they exist at some troubled interface of self and environment. As paradoxical as Winnicott's 'transitional object', they neither belong unproblematically to the subject nor may they be decisively repudiated as 'not-me'; like the image in the mirror they constitute a scandalous reminder that the subject is never fully present to him or herself. Nothing could be more menacing to the precariously self-possessed classicist: not only must the bodily product itself be repressed from consciousness, but also the sense that libidinally delighted in it, and accordingly *all* strong smells become dangerous allusions to these forbidden pleasures and the bewildering psychic 'space' in which they took place.[20]

'Sweeney Erect' itself does not so much renounce as *amputate* the tabooed areas of subjectivity that the woman represents, though the text remains coy about the link between the woman's convulsions and Sweeney's gesture of testing the razor on his leg. Yet Doris's entry in the final stanza has something of the hieratic ritualism of the priestess bearing libations at a sacrifice, as well as the routine efficiency of the surgeon's assistant administering an anaesthetic: entering just as the poem itself exits, she suggests a narrative beyond the letter of the text. In one sense the poem evades the issue. By making the woman an epileptic, the terrific violence it evokes becomes a biological visitation divorced from human agency. But at the same time a phantasy of carving flesh with a razor-like implement penetrates the very description of the woman's body: 'the *sickle* motion from the thighs/*Jackknifes* upward' (*CP*, p. 44 – emphasis added). She is effectively a patient upon a table, though at this point an unetherised one. Sweeney may indeed be based on a Boston pugilist of Eliot's acquaintance, but he is first and foremost Sweeney Todd, the London barber with a more than professional enthusiasm for razor-wielding and a relish, exemplified in his notorious pies, for oral incorporation of the morsels of his victims.

The 'broadbottomed' Sweeney of this poem makes a subsequent brief appearance shifting 'from ham to ham . . . in his bath' at the close of 'Mr Eliot's Sunday Morning Service' (*CP*, p. 58). This curious vignette is illuminated by the Aeschylean epigraph to 'Sweeney among the Nightingales': 'Alas, I am struck deep with a mortal blow.' This is the cry of Agamemnon, struck down by his wife Clytemnestra as he bathes in a silver cauldron after his triumphant return from the Trojan war. It is a crucial moment in Eliot's poetry, marking the point where the stairs motif of *Crime and Punishment*, which had been the structuring phantasy of the early verse, gives way to his long fascination with Aeschylus's *Oresteia*, which will play a similar role in his later work. The reciprocal violences of the early poetry are now cast as a narrative: Aeschylus's trilogy opens with the murder of the husband by a wife as formidable as Eliot's Grishkin – 'couched Brazilian jaguar' to Agamemnon's 'scampering marmoset' (*CP*, p. 55) – but reaches a later climax with the bloody revenging of that murder by Orestes. I shall discuss the play and Melanie Klein's unfinished essay on it more fully later in relation to Eliot's *Family Reunion*, whose disruptive subtext it constitutes. For the moment it is sufficient to note the shadow the play casts over Sweeney splashing in his bath, and it may be the reminiscence of Clytemnestra's mutilating attack that explains the unlikely affinity Eliot implies between Sweeney and 'The masters of the subtle schools' (*CP*, p. 58). For the most subtle polymath of them all was 'enervate Origen', self-castrated to purify his thought.

'Sweeney among the Nightingales' (*CP*, pp. 59–60) is also cowed by its fearsome Aeschylean epigraph. Erect as ever, Sweeney is nevertheless much more on the defensive than before; he must now guard 'the hornèd gate', and the adjective bears upon us in its colloquial as well as its classical connotations. This is also true of the poem itself, which begins energetically enough in an attempt to repeat the physical grotesquerie of 'Sweeney Erect', but then unaccountably fades into the monotonous syntax, the wearily uninspired vocabulary, of its central stanzas, where the text itself is as fatigued as the man in mocha brown. The early rhetorical attempt to swell Sweeney to heroic status trails out, and it is the women in the poem who mobilise the more effective and sinister violence; 'Rachel *née* Rabinovitch/Tears at the grapes with murderous paws' in a ravening display of oral vindictiveness. If Sweeney is Agamemnon, then the man in mocha brown is not 'a modern hero returning at the end of the 1914–18 war', as A. D. Moody suggests,[21] but rather the treacherous, if languid, Aegisthus, conspiring with the poem's assorted Clytemnestras to bring about its protagonist's bloody downfall.

The 'someone indistinct' with whom the host converses at the door is something like a textual unconscious, the impinging trace of an Aeschylean subtext or phantasy that is about to erupt from the repressed:

> The nightingales are singing near
> The Convent of the Sacred Heart,

And sang within the bloody wood
When Agamemnon cried aloud
And let their liquid siftings fall
To stain the stiff dishonoured shroud.

(*CP*, p. 60)

The nightingales or whores drown out the voices of the nuns in the convent, as the idealised maternal imago succumbs to its bad sexualised counterpart. This latter adds its 'liquid siftings' as an anal component to Rachel's oral sadism, and *Poems 1920* thus ends with Sweeney ironically besmeared with the very faeces it had been the purpose of Eliot's stress on his upright stance to repress. 'Sweeney among the Nightingales' forms a pendant to 'Sweeney Erect', the two poems together enacting in reverse the veering power relationships of 'The Love Song of Saint Sebastian'. And such psychic instabilities may appear in miniature in the structure of meaning of a single word, as in the '*snarled* and yelping seas' of 'Sweeney Erect' (*CP*, p. 44; emphasis added). The image evoked by 'yelping' forces its neighbouring epithet towards its more actively aggressive sense of 'snarling', while the word as given equally insists on its own thwarted passivity; it has somehow become tangled in its own aggressiveness.

Ending up flat on his back and caked with bird's droppings, Sweeney Erect might seem to have outlived his poetic usefulness for Eliot, and to mark the abandonment, at the end of *Poems 1920*, of the latter's attempt to follow the classicist footsteps of Hulme and Pound. But in fact the character makes an energetic return some years later in *Sweeney Agonistes*, where, as Doris aptly remarks, 'A woman runs a terrible risk' (*CP*, p. 134). This forthright facing of violent impulses towards the female is already a notable departure in the Eliot canon. Doris negotiates a precarious path between Sweeney's desire to turn her into a 'nice little . . . missionary stew' and the alternative fate, sketched in Sweeney's tale of a man he once knew, of being 'done in' and preserved 'With a gallon of lysol in a bath' (*CP*, pp. 130, 134). Having just drawn 'the COFFIN very last card', she cannot feel quite the enthusiasm for Sweeney's narrative that Snow and Swarts do. Eliot struggled with the fragments of the play for years, but could never finish it. In explanation of this commentators have usually suggested either that Eliot was afflicted with some innate dramatic incapacity or that his theme was somehow inherently unsuited to the stage. Eliot's difficulty seems to me to reside rather in the incompatibility of the psychic strategies announced by the play's epigraphs. Unable either to renounce or reconcile them, the text flounders about a while between the two options and then gives up, resigning itself to the status of a poetic lame duck.

'Hence the soul cannot be possessed of the divine union, until it has divested itself of the love of created beings', counsels St John of the Cross (*CP*, p. 121). Since the creation in question is God's rather than the self's, the phrase 'created things' acknowledges the autonomy of the objective world, but only to call for a regression from this depressive insight to the more primitive fusion of self and other that is divine union. In Freudian terms, St John is advising a withdrawal of the libidinal cathexis of the external world and the return of the freed libido to its original reservoir, primary narcissism.[22] But the play itself interprets divine union as a Kleinian process in Sweeney's parody of the Eucharist: oral incorporation of the good object. 'I'll gobble you up. I'll be the cannibal', he enthuses to Doris, and the cannibalistic imagery casts its sombre shadow back over the 'dull tom-tom' beaten out in 'Portrait of a Lady' (*CP*, pp. 130, 19). However, this omnipotent phantasy of union with the good object proves impossible to sustain. Sweeney's frenetic rhythms suggest that the intense idealisation of Doris as a luminous 'Gauguin maid' (*CP*, p. 132) involves an excessive expenditure of psychic energy. The ego proves to have too developed a capacity for reality-testing to be partner to a manic denial of the autonomous world of telephones and Rolls Royces in favour of Sweeney's phantasy of a tropical island with 'nothing to hear but the sound of the surf (*CP*, p. 131). Moreover, Doris too refuses to co-operate: 'I'd be bored', she complains, or (*CP*, p. 130), insisting on her role as missionary rather than stew, 'I'll convert you' (and so she will, not in this play but in *Ash-Wednesday*). Created things are altogether more importunate than St John of the Cross ever imagined, resisting and subverting the manipulations planned for them by the paranoid–schizoid ego.

Perhaps Orestes then, who is the source of the play's second epigraph, will prove a more helpful spiritual guide, and the yearned for divine union may be better attained by his methods, which include putting his mother to death with a sword. Such, in effect, is the burden of Sweeney's tale of a man he once knew, a man who need not be strictly distinguished from Sweeney himself because

> Any man has to, needs to, wants to
> Once in a lifetime, do a girl in.
> (*CP*, p. 134)

Eliot's poetic *oeuvre* may be regarded as a rich set of elaborations on the possibilities of those two lines, although when confronted with them by an audience of Vassar students after a performance of *Sweeney Agonistes*, he politely demurred: 'his disavowal of having himself done a girl in (at least up to May, 1933) is a matter of public record. . . . He stated that he was not the type.'[23] Right type or not, doing a girl in may anyway not achieve its desired end: the murderer whose tale Sweeney tells does not get pinched, but nor does he attain the divine union. Such merging of subject and object as does take place is a hideous travesty of that goal:

> He didn't know if he was alive
> and the girl was dead
> He didn't know if the girl was alive
> and he was dead
> (*CP*, p. 135)

His fate is more like that of Orestes, whose violence returns upon himself in the persecutory phantasies that Aeschylus represents as the Furies; hence the second epigraph: 'You don't see them, you don't – but *I* see them: they are hunting me down, I must move on' (*CP*, p. 121).

But the full consequences of the Oresteian situation are avoided in this tale, and this fact also suggests why Eliot could not complete the play. Orestes's persecution by the Furies involves not only fear of retaliation, but also grief, guilt, acceptance of responsibility for his act of destruction. It has a strong depressive component; and the reparative superego mourns and seeks to reconstitute the damaged object. This drive towards reparation propels Orestes and the narrative of the drama itself to a beneficent conclusion under Athena, who yokes the Furies to the maintenance of a new social order. In *Sweeney Agonistes*, however, there is no reparation and hence no sustained narrative. 'Is it perfume from a dress / That makes me so digress?' Prufrock had already wondered (*CP*, p. 15), suggesting that paranoid–schizoid proximity to the female body and narrative continuity are incompatible. Depressive reparation proposes a goal – the restored good object – and can therefore accommodate the teleological dispositions of narrative. But in *Sweeney Agonistes* full admission of violence is evaded by a gallon of lysol, a neat device of manic denial whereby the corpse is preserved 'for a couple of months' after death (*CP*, p. 134). It becomes the mere sign of a woman, given 'in remembrance' of a presence that is henceforth always deferred. But the paradox of this corpse is that it is a mere substitute that none the less bestows a fuller presence than its original ever did. No longer as obstreperous as Doris, yielding itself entirely to the subject's phantasy, the corpse allows the perfect 'mutuality' it had always frustrated in life. As a Derridean supplement that ousts its object, the dead body defies exposition in Sweeney's binary logic, which, in these fraught cases, 'don't apply'; the principle of self-identity has no purchase here, for both murderer and victim are 'either or neither' at once (*CP*, p. 135). Fear of retaliation is now displaced onto such eminently reasonable objects of concern as neighbours or rent-collectors, or returns only in Raskolnikovian nightmares when 'you wake like someone hit you in the head' (*CP*, p. 136). Floating in her bath, the dead woman testifies that Clytemnestra's murderousness has been deftly turned back upon herself. She also recalls Prufrock's mermaids, submarine women deliciously compliant to the protagonist's needs. In so far as the girl in the bath is recognised as dead, *Sweeney Agonistes* advances beyond the more whimsical phantasy; but the pickled afterlife it grants its devastated object prevents the more radical break into Oresteian reparation. St John and Orestes are odd bedfellows, and the text finally runs aground on the incompatibility of its epigraphs. Sweeney is too committed to the autonomous reality of his object (Doris) to manhandle it in a phantasy oral incorporation that would secure mystical union, but, as soon as his Oresteian violence is provoked by that resistant object, he finds himself too fixated in paranoid-schizoid mechanisms of denial to cope with depressive pain. Caught on the horns of that hopeless dilemma, Eliot simply abandoned the theme for the fifteen years that divide this play from *The Family Reunion*.

The final text for consideration in the context of Eliot's allegiance to the Pound–Lewis–Hulme axis of English modernism is 'Coriolan', a poem he was working on in the early 1930s but which finally proved as intractable as his play about Sweeney and which joins that play in the category of 'Unfinished Poems' in the *Collected Poems* of 1936. Dealing directly with the over-investment in the carving-tradition and depressive separating out that

characterises the classicist-modernists, 'Coriolan' gratifyingly
conforms to a Kleinian or Stokesian interpretation, but is for that
very reason less poetically interesting than many of its predecessors.
Its hero is Shakespeare's Coriolanus, who at one point in his career
seeks to repudiate his own mother and stand alone as if author of his
own being; but he is also Ezra Pound's Sigismondo Malatesta or
Benito Mussolini or even the *Führer* himself. What he is not,
however, is the 'broken Coriolanus' of *The Waste Land* (*CP*, p.
79). Rigidly refusing all interchange with its environment, his is as
opaque and uninterrogative a gaze as any in Eliot. As tensely self-
involved as he is indifferent to the crowd, his will is focused
inwards to resist the encroachments of the maternal enticements –
'O hidden under the dove's wing' – which threaten the 'natural
wakeful life of our Ego' (*CP*, pp. 140, 139). It remains unclear
whether these lyrical interludes articulate the commander's yen to
lapse out into the mother's protection, or whether, on the
contrary, his impenetrability provides that Winnicottian
satisfaction for the crowds, just as the imperious will of Amy
Monchensey creates a parody of the Eliotic still point in *The Family
Reunion*. A related ambiguity surrounds the rituals over which the
commander presides. On the one hand, the virgins 'go up' to the
temple, presumably mounting the Raskolnikovian staircase, and
return with 'urns containing/Dust' or the incinerated good object
(*CP*, p. 140); the sacrifices are thus the culmination of the military
parade, consigning the tabooed, 'feminine' areas of the psyche to
ashes. But, on the other hand, Coriolan expects these very rituals to
secure union with the mother; may we not be together, he
implores, 'If the mactations . . . are now observed' (*CP*, p. 142).
Hopelessly self-divided and without the Roman strength of will
that enabled his ancestors to bear what Winnicott terms 'the strain
inherent in objective perception' (*PR*, p. 16), Coriolan is a mere
psychic cripple. The 'RESIGN RESIGN RESIGN' that closes the
poem passes a judgement on him as decisive as the 'liquid siftings'
that spatter Agamemnon–Sweeney's shroud at the end of *Poems
1920* (*CP*, pp. 143, 60).

   Clive Bell, himself no friend to Hulme and Pound, once described
Renaissance art as 'a big kink in a long slope', an impressive but
misguided detour from the authentic traditions of medieval painting
which contemporary Post-Impressionism had retrieved.[24]
Something similar might be said of Eliot's attempt to attach himself
to the 'carving' tradition of modernist poetry. One or two provisos

must at once be made. It is not a question of a principle of evil (carving, classicism, Pound) supervening brutally from the outside upon an innocent 'modeller'; 'Portrait of a Lady', one of Eliot's finest carved texts, was written long before his connections with Imagism and Pound. Nor was Eliot ever unreservedly committed to his classicist kink. 'The Death of Saint Narcissus' subverts its classicist pedigree; 'Mr Apollinax' holds open a shy space for Fragilion; Sweeny comes to an excremental end or, like Coriolan, ruins by rendering unfinishable the major text in which he appears. A sense persists throughout these texts that the poet is working against the psychic grain, but the detour, if 'misguided', is productive too. Without attaching himself to the brash energies of literary classicism like Ulysses to his sheep's belly, Eliot would never have escaped the Cyclopean terrors of the paranoid–schizoid long enough to celebrate that memorable 'carver' Sweeney Erect.

4 Not Waving but Drowning: *The Waste Land* to Eliot's Drama

As everyone now knows, *The Waste Land* was drafted in 1921 during Eliot's convalescence from some kind of nervous breakdown due to overwork, financial worries, tension with his family back in America, and the prolonged strains of his disastrous marriage. This list could probably be extended, but will not in itself explain why the crisis should have occurred precisely when it did. Casting around for precipitating causes, one comes upon the inescapable fact that Eliot's collapse immediately followed his mother's first and long-awaited visit to England. How deeply that visit was necessary to him is suggested by a letter to his brother in 1920 (*WLF*, p. xviii) where Eliot's heavy, repeated stress on *seeing* the mother has the resonant quality of Hegelian recognition rather than denoting mere visual proximity. That aspiration, I shall argue below, will be denied in *The Waste Land* itself by the sea-change that turns Phlebas's eyes to pearl. Details of Mrs Eliot's visit in 1921 are not available, yet it is nevertheless clear that Eliot had radically underestimated his mother's strength and vitality. Since she was seventy-seven years old, he anticipated that physical frailty would render her visit more an anxiety than a joy to him. But in the event he was to find her energy no less than terrifying (*WLF*, p. xxi). If the son had been expecting a reversal of that equally dramatic encounter with the mother in Boston in 1910 when she had nursed him back to health after a 'mysterious' illness, if he now expected to nurse her, his expectations were wide of the mark indeed. Even on that earlier occasion she had, after all, nursed him through a neurosis of which she may have been a major contributory factor, and a decade later she again appears to have precipitated her son into nervous disorder. Whereas he had expected Charlotte Champe Eliot to be an endear-

94

ingly docile angel, she actually turned out to be a most formidable octopus.

That disquieting experience may have played its part in Eliot's first choice of an epigraph for *The Waste Land*, the lines from *Heart of Darkness* which recount Kurtz's death and culminate in his cry, 'The horror! The horror!' This epigraph was later deleted on Pound's advice, though Eliot rebelliously murmured that it was 'much the most appropriate I can find, and somewhat elucidative' (*WLF*, p. 125). In its reference to Kurtz living 'his life again in every detail of desire, temptation and surrender', the Conradian epigraph stresses the anguished subjective origins of the text, undercutting its pretensions to an impersonal survey of cultural decay. But whether its desires, temptations and surrenders are, as has occasionally been suggested, the homosexual ones offered by Mr Eugenides may be doubted. If the rejected epigraph is indeed 'elucidative', it must be given its *full* weight, for *Heart of Darkness* too has its octopus and angel. There is first the magnificent negress who has apparently been Kurtz's mistress during his rule in the African jungle, and this 'couched Brazilian jaguar' of a woman is paired in the tale with Kurtz's idealised Intended: 'her forehead, smooth and white, remained illumined by the inextinguishable light of belief and love'.[1] Here again, then, is the familiar world of primitive internal objects and their attendant mechanisms of splitting and idealisation. In narrative situation too the tale has its resemblance to Eliot's verse; its journey up the Congo, like Eliot's ascent of the staircase, is a penetration into the maternal body. More impressive still for Eliot, perhaps, are the intimations of cannibalism that lurk behind the portentous murkiness of Conrad's rhetoric: 'unspeakable secrets' and 'abominable satisfactions' whet our literary appetites for a full revelation that never comes. These are surely the desires, temptations and surrenders that prompt Kurtz's final cry and that mark his elucidative value for Eliot's poem. For, after the Sweeney poems with their more or less unsuccessful venture into the depressive position, *The Waste Land* constitutes a regression – with a vengeance – to the paranoid–schizoid.

One further artistic influence on the poem is apposite here: Stravinsky's *Le Sacre du Printemps*. At one level that work merely reinforced a lesson Eliot had already absorbed from Frazer's *Golden Bough*: transforming 'the rhythm of the steppes into the scream of the motor-horn' (*EEY*, p. 108), it too affirmed the continuity of the modern mind with its primitive forbears. But the ballet's effect may have sunk deeper even than that. The *Sacre*, with its climactic dance to sacrificial death of the chosen virgin, has a close affinity with T. E. Hulme's 'The Sunset'; and so involved did Eliot become in the performance of the ballet he attended that he set about his laughing neighbours in the audience with the point of his umbrella, an act that is oblique confirmation of the violence that I argued was latent in the 'sinister murmurs' of the Hulme poem. Theodor Adorno has argued that the condition of enjoying the liquidation of Stravinsky's young dancer is an analogous sacrifice of the listener's own subjectivity to the archaic rhythms of the music itself.[2] Such sado-masochism, a Pyrrhic victory over the object because the subject will himself be implicated in the devastation, will be a significant feature of *The Waste Land*.

Focusing on the original epigraph to the poem does not, however, merely abolish the one it now carries: 'For once I saw with my very own eyes the Sybil at Cumae hanging in a cage, and when the boys said to her, "Sybil, what do you want?", she answered, "I want to die." ' Here again is the narrative situation familiar from 'The Sunset' or *Le Sacre du Printemps*: a male audience marshalled against its female victim. The aggression of the former is successfully denied by projection, attributed rather to the aged Sybil's own death-wish than to the taunts of the Greek boys, in much the way that Pound's Daphne welcomed her own immobilisation. Yet, while it obligingly conforms to my specific theme, this epigraph may also have general consequences for the interpretation of *The Waste Land*. Its source is Petronius's *Satyricon*, a work that also provided Eliot with the epigraph to *The Sacred Wood* and whose detailed links with the poem have been carefully traced by F. N. Lees. It is not, however, to these particular debts but to the *generic* implications of the *Satyricon* for *The Waste Land* that I wish to draw attention. For Petronius's text is one of the founding instances of the traditional genre (or anti-genre) of the *menippea*, which is characterised by its

> hostility to static, discrete units . . . its juxtaposition of incompatible elements and its resistance to fixity. Spatial, temporal, and philosophical ordering systems all dissolve; unified notions of character are broken; language and syntax become incoherent. . . . Unable to give affirmation to a closed, unified, or omniscient vision, the *menippea* violates social propriety. It tells of descents into underworlds of brothels, prisons,

orgies, graves: it has no fear of the criminal, erotic, mad, or dead.[3]

In his *Problems of Dostoevsky's Poetics* Mikhail Bakhtin links *menippea* to the notion of carnival, for, if the former gleefully turns literary decorum inside out, the latter does the same for the sobre routines and structures of everyday life. The Petronian epigraph to *The Waste Land* thus retroactively makes my invocation of Bakhtinian carnival in relation to 'Hysteria' and 'Portrait of a Lady' less arbitrary than it may originally have seemed.

But it is less in its violation of social taboo by scavenging for subject-matter among the detritus of brothels, prisons and graves, and more in its *formal* dislocations, that the *menippea* is most subversive: binary oppositions crash to the ground, the 'organic unity' of the text is brazenly flouted, unitary notions of character slip, slide and perish, the narrative point of view is busily unravelled into an unresolvable plurality of conflicting voices. In a note to *The Waste Land* Eliot points out that Mr Eugenides 'melts into' Phlebas the Phoenician, who in turn is 'not wholly distinct' from Ferdinand, Prince of Naples (*CP*, p. 82). To this degree the poem takes up the campaign he had announced in 'Tradition and the Individual Talent' against 'the metaphysical theory of the substantial unity of the soul' (*SE*, p. 19), and lends literary weight to Bradley's claim that the ego is not ultimately real. But what Eliot concedes with one hand to the vertiginous slippages and slidings of *menippea* he at once takes back with the other. Tiresias is 'the most important personage in the poem, uniting all the rest' (*CP*, p. 82), and the invocation of textual *unity* betrays the text's nostalgia for a master synthesis that would somehow gather in the radically disparate and unstable fragments it is composed of. This tension recurs at the level of the sign itself: the poem's tendency to romp wildly across the pastures of the European vernaculars suffers a *rappel à l'ordre* in the heavy Sanskrit intonations of its close. Like Tiresias, Sanskrit is a textual master code, folding back the splintered vernaculars into a primal source of self-present meaning.

Eliot's own hesitancy between menippean licence and organicist conservatism is replayed in the 'homosexual' interpretation of his text. In terms of content this reading is the most scandalous yet produced; Eliot himself threatened to sue its originator, John Peter, and it has yet to emerge fully from the embarrassed silence that first confronted it. But *formally* this view is as conservative as Tiresias himself. John Peter and James Miller invoke menippean fluidity to 'prove' that the hyacinth girl, if we had only looked a little closer and lifted the textual fig-leaf, was actually a boy, but overall they assign the poem to the category of dramatic monologue. Governed by a single, unitary consciousness, the poem will sustain a narrative adventure as shapely in its teleology as a Victorian novel. Admittedly it is a little ragged, but we can always 'fill in for ourselves some of the "story" ', plugging and patching the text as we go.[4]

Undoubtedly no interpretation can proceed without its transcendental signifier, whether that signifier is homosexuality or the 'abyss' that would deny all transcendental signification; but since John Peter wrote in 1951 the interpretative waters have become even murkier. Composed as it is of a tissue of citations from other texts, *The Waste Land* has always undermined unitary readings: what you pulled out of one source could always be matched by the contradictory implications of another, and the hermeneutic problem was anyway only pushed one stage further back into the difficulty of interpreting the source text in the first place. To go to the sources in quest of a semantic authority that would leave Eliot's poem formulated, pinned and wriggling on the critic's wall in fact only led to a further spiral of interpretation; *The Waste Land*'s sources do not enjoy the primal command over their 'derivatives' that Sanskrit possesses. With the publication in 1971 of the *Waste Land* facsimile the whole problem begins to get out of hand. What now is the relation of this fascinating tangle of drafts to the public text that emerges out of Pound's editing? And what of that editing itself? While many of Pound's excisions are undoubted stylistic gains (but what in this context are the criteria behind such judgements?), it is also clear that he had deleted whole passages that at least match anything he allowed to remain. There could, anyway, hardly be a more 'compromised' editor than Pound himself. I have already suggested some of the tensions in the literary relations between Eliot and Pound in the case of the Hamlet paragraph in 'Prufrock', and my last chapter argues Pound's profound implication in the kind of Kleinian issues *The Waste Land* epigraphs adumbrate. What is now needed is a study of the editing of the drafts that would consider it as a Poundian psychoanalytic 'text' in its own right.

By diligent probing of the poem's citations and by reinstating material from the manuscripts, the interpreter can now have his or her sport with *The Waste Land* in any way, shape or form. Any new reading of the text must therefore make decisions on these matters which are better articulated than merely implicit. In what follows I have chosen to give considerable attention to the long narrative of a fishing-expedition which Pound deleted from 'Death by Water'. This was one of his most savage cuts; of the original ninety lines only eight survive, as the description of the drowned Phlebas. Editorially it was an odd decision. Unlike the long passages about Fresca and Boston nightlife, which were deleted in their entirety, enough of the fishing-narrative escapes the censor to hint tantalisingly at what might once have been. It is thus a scar or fold in the text, the trace of editorial violence and the implication of a depth which the poem as it stands cannot altogether sustain. Restoring this death by water to its full status may in turn allow a bringing into full critical consciousness of the scene of a second drowning – of an Ophelia or a hyacinth girl – which the text can never quite articulate, ultimately flinching away from it at every nervous approach. This phantasmatic supplement, as Bersani predicted, will clamorously announce its absence-presence by a 'high visibility of significant lacks', and *The Waste Land*, now as scarred by its own repressions as it was mutilated by Ezra Pound, may fittingly take its place within the psychoanalytic reading of Eliot's *oeuvre* that I am here proposing.

Eliot's assertion that Tiresias is 'the most important personage in the poem, uniting all the rest. . . . the two sexes meet in Tiresias' (*CP*, p. 82) indicates that his importance is not only a matter of his impersonal, prophetic authority but also of his bisexuality. Whereas in Greek myth Tiresias was successively male and female, in *The Waste Land* he is explicitly hermaphroditic: 'old man with wrinkled dugs' (*CP*, p. 72). One reason for this is that Tiresias is 'not wholly distinct' from the death-desiring Sybil of the poem's epigraph, whose longevity and powers of prophecy rival his own. His hermaphroditism also unites the two crucial figures of the text, whom I shall refer to in their guises as the drowned Ophelia and the drowned Phlebas. If the latter picks up an earlier comparison of Sweeney to Agamemnon murdered in his bath, the former looks forward to the girl in *Sweeney Agonistes* who floats in her gallon of lysol; the number of deaths by (or in) water in Eliot thus doubles at a stroke. The accidents of his career allow Tiresias to contain both (or all four) of these figures, and, composed as he is of dead or dying objects, it is small wonder that he appears rather as symptom than diagnostician of the moribund civilisation he surveys.

Blind as well as epicene, Tiresias is also linked with the symbolically castrated Fisher King; both characters feature in the poem for the first time in 'The Fire Sermon'. The causes of Tiresias's blindness may therefore throw light on the unexplained sterility of his counterpart. After supporting Jove against Juno in his claim that women enjoyed the greater pleasure in sex, Tiresias was struck blind by the latter, though he was later granted the power of prophecy and long life by Jove in compensation. Juno's aggression confirms the formidable sexuality Tiresias attributed to her and to women generally, and she emerges as a mythic precursor of the dangerously sexual and castrating imago evoked in Eliot's 'Circe'. Ironically, it is Tiresias's very effort to identify with the father by supporting Jove's argument that provokes Juno's emasculating attack and puts an untimely end to his attempt to work through the Oedipus complex. Juno may stand as a type of the mother who 'denies the speech of the father its function as law . . . prevents the child from acceding to the paternal metaphor' (*JL*, p. 235), and, while the myth allows the paternal law to be reaffirmed at a higher level (foresight rather than sight), *The Waste Land* remains unconvinced. Tiresias may have gained his oracular abilities, but the castrated Fisher King fishes on disconsolately with the arid plain behind him.

The latter is confronted with the poem's most vivid tactile evocation of Sartre's *le visqueux* as a rat drags 'its slimy belly' across the bank on which he fishes:

> Musing upon the king my brother's wreck
> And on the king my father's death before him.
> (*CP*, p. 70)

With Pound's excision of the fishing and shipwreck narrative of 'Death by Water', this passage loses much of its premonitory force. *The Tempest* furnishes no brother to account for the Fisher King's reference, and in view of his shared plight of symbolic castration Tiresias emerges as the likeliest candidate for this unfilled fraternal office. If the Tiresias myth furnishes a dangerous mother and a toppled father, *The Tempest* then affords a narrative situation that consigns the latter to a watery fate. Crossbreed the Shakespearean and classical allusions – a textual fusion for which we have the poet's authority since Tiresias 'unites all the rest' – and the figures of Agamemnon and Clytemnestra, crucial to both *Sweeney Agonistes* and *The Family Reunion*, stand forth. The king–father is thus effaced, toppled by a mother who has denied his speech its function as law, and the brooding Fisher King and his blind 'brother' Tiresias partake of his defeat: condemned to represent the phallus for the mother, they do not in any real sense possess it themselves and are to that extent castrated. At the same time, however, they are also the avenging Orestes, violently disposed to wrest the phallus away from the mother. After butchering Clytemnestra, Orestes is both pursued by the persecutory Erinyes and prompted by impulses of reparation which will ultimately transform those pursuers into the benevolent Eumenides. I shall argue that the absent centre of *The Waste Land* is precisely an Oresteian phantasy of attack on the mother. While the poem cannot finally escape the paranoid–schizoid position, because it will not fully acknowledge that assault, it does none the less open under the aegis of a tentative impulse to reparation.

The pain of the opening lines – aching roots stirred into reluctant life by the cruellest month – is surely a depressive pain, a chink in a previously blanketing repression; if the dead are indeed to be buried, it must not be by any strategy of manic denial but rather in full acknowledgement of the psyche's own sadistic impulses. Only then will fertility be restored to a self at present composed of 'stony rubbish' and 'broken images' (*CP*, p. 63) a waste land of dead internal objects. First imaged by the promptings of the seasonal cycle, the drive to reparation becomes more urgent still in the second section of 'Burial of the Dead'. The prophetic voice represents the superego in its depressive aspect, systematically dissociating itself from its primitive and persecutory predecessors; it is neither

> Your shadow at morning striding behind you
> Or your shadow at evening rising to meet you . . .
> (*CP*, pp. 63–4)

Instead it proposes to 'show you fear in a handful of dust', a fear that is allied more to guilt than to terror of retaliation and which at once leads the poem to the hyacinth girl.

Yet this is not the first time fear has entered the text. As the April stirrings undo the work of denial, dissolving 'forgetful snow', they have already thrown up the memory of Marie staying at her cousin's, the archduke:

> he took me out on a sled,
> And I was frightened. He said, Marie,
> Marie, hold on tight. And down we went.
>
> (*CP*, p. 63)

'Regressive thrills', comments Hugh Kenner in one of the few assessments the lines have ever received, and he is surely right; but just *who* is regressing here? Marie's fear seems to me more serious than Kenner allows; a woman, as we know, runs a terrible risk. Women in physical motion have a certain fascination for Eliot. On the one hand, there is an awed excitement at the unleashing outwards of that secret inner energy that had seemed to seethe and ferment *inside* the female body: Cousin Nancy 'Strode across the hills and broke them' with something of the phallic dynamism of Apollinax himself (*CP*, p. 32). But, on the other, there is also 'Priapus in the shrubbery/Gaping at the lady in the swing' (*CP*, p. 33). Preoccupied as she now is with matters of balance requiring her full attention, the woman is a hapless victim of the male's shamelessly voyeuristic gaze; in the accidents of activity and motion she may expose parts of herself that otherwise remain decorously covered. On faster-moving vessels or vehicles she is more vulnerable still, for she may always tumble off, particularly if, like Harry in *The Family Reunion*, you are there to give her a helping shove. Marie's sled is an example of this third kind of female motion, and its risks may be suggested by noting the network of verbal anticipations in which they are stitched. The archduke's counsel to hold on tight looks forward to the fingers of leaf that 'Clutch and sink into the wet bank' (*CP*, p. 70), where a desperate grip does not escape its autumnal fate. Marie's own 'down we went' would be an equally apt cry from either the drowning Ophelia or the shipwrecked mariners of the original 'Death by Water', and as a landscape of terror the snow-covered Alps down which she sleds has much in common with the iceberg against which the sailors shatter. As 'Memory and desire' stir (*CP*, p. 63), an *Ur*-version of the text's phantasmatic supplement is cast up, and the problem posed of its relationship to the subsequent episode in the hyacinth garden.

The hyacinths are perhaps a symbol of the resurrected god of the fertility rites, but as far as the text is concerned they connote a distant hope rather than an achieved actuality. For its restorative impulse is precarious. It was the Sybil, burdened by an unimaginable span of years, who pleaded for death, not the Greek boys who wanted to dispatch her. Marie's fear is similarly naturalised, implicitly attributed to the risks of sledding rather than the sinister presence of the archduke. Shaken but not dislodged, manic denial still operates powerfully, and the nature of events in the hyacinth garden remains desperately obscure. When they came back, late,

> Your arms full, and your hair wet, I could not
> Speak, and my eyes failed, I was neither
> Living nor dead, and I knew nothing,
> Looking into the heart of light, the silence.'
>
> (*CP*, p. 64)

Formally, the passage constitutes a riposte to the poem's opening lines. Whereas there the verbs of natural quickening groped painfully but with a dogged hopefulness across the line-endings to encounter their objects, here the words of significant human process – 'Speak', 'Living', 'Looking' – are displaced from that position by resounding negatives. The best comments on these lines are Hugh Kenner's. Pointing to the blank card that Madame Sosostris draws, to the 'something which he carries on his back, / Which I am forbidden to see', he remarks, 'In what posture did they come back, late, from the Hyacinth Garden, her hair wet, before the planting of the corpse? It is not clear whether he is comforted to learn that the clairvoyante does not find the Hanged Man.'[5]

The hyacinth garden is so central to its text and the interpretation of it so much a crux in the criticism of Eliot that it pays to linger over the issues it raises. Bernard Bergonzi's account is typical: it constitutes 'a shared experience, whose intensity can be conveyed, but which can be neither described nor explained. To this extent, we are encountering the symbolist method of *The Waste Land*.'[6] Symbolism is ritually invoked as criticism lapses into vacuity, throwing up its hands before the ineffable. But the text itself is aware that more is at stake than this as it refers to areas of itself that it is 'forbidden to see'. In this sense Symbolism is no more than one of the text's evasive strategies: if it can persuade us that its blindness is actually the dazzle of the Symbol, dark with excessive light, then the heresy of paraphrase and with it Kenner's awkward questions will have been ruled firmly out of bounds. The Symbolist critic merely colludes with the text's own psychic defence. I have already suggested that Eliot's early Gothicism be allowed to problematise his Symbolist affiliations, and his own praise of Gottfried Benn later in his life implies an affinity with the psychic extremism of the Expressionist movement that Mallarmé and Valéry may tend to obscure. It is, ironically, this very hyacinth passage, where we are supposedly 'encountering the symbolist method of *The Waste Land*', that will make that affinity decisively clear.

Whether Eliot had ever seen or read *The Ghost Sonata* (1907) by Johan August Strindberg I do not know, but its parallels to *The Waste Land* are striking. Strindberg's Old Man does not quite match Tiresias for longevity, but he none the less has the power of prophecy and is linked with that deeply Eliotic motif, the drowning woman: 'Although I am not a Sunday child, yet I possess the gift of prophecy, and also the gift of healing. I once summoned a drowning girl back to life.'[7] This reparative claim turns out to be a lie. Bengtsson informs us later that the Old Man had in fact 'lured a young girl out on the ice to drown her' (p. 181); he thus shares an enthusiasm with the man whose tale Sweeney tells, for he too is more concerned with holding women under water than with helping them clamber out. It is the final scene of Strindberg's play that is most relevant to Eliot's hyacinth garden. We have been prepared, as in *The Tempest*, for a romantic reconciliation in the new generation that will wipe away the evils and enmities of the old; the Student and Daughter meet in a room with 'hyacinths of all colours, everywhere':

DAUGHTER. Sing for my flowers.
STUDENT. Is the hyacinth your flower?
DAUGHTER. It is my only flower. You love the hyacinth, too?
STUDENT. Above all other flowers . . . I have loved hyacinths
    ever since I was a child. I have worshipped them, because
    they embody everything I lack. And yet –   (p. 183)

Already the encounter is shot through with uneasiness, and both the optimism and the imminent failure of the relationship are expressed in imagery remarkably close to Eliot's lines on April and on the sensory failure that follows the return from the hyacinth garden. Strindberg's Student continues, 'Their perfume, strong and clean with the first zephyrs of spring, which have passed over melting snow, confuses my senses, deafens me, blinds me, drives me from my room, shoots me with poisoned arrows' (p. 183). The reason for this breakdown is the alarming presence of the Cook, an ogress obscurely related to the text's Tiresias-like Old Man. Her 'service' is a merciless expression of oral sadism and vampiric torment: 'She boils the meat till it is nothing but sinews and water, while she herself drinks the juice from it. When she roasts she cooks the meat till the goodness is gone; she drinks the gravy and the blood' (p. 185). In her lurid monstrosity she is the obverse of the idealised Daughter, whose living pith is drained to the point of death by this horrific attendant, who puts even the gobbling, cavernous throat of Eliot's 'Hysteria' quite in the shade. Strindberg's undergraduate Perseus cannot save his Andromeda from the dragon, and the play closes with a prayer for peace and release in Buddhist accents not far removed from the Sanskrit chant that concludes *The Waste Land.*

There are, then, distinguished precedents for a death among the hyacinths, and in a context that bears a close relationship to the misogynistic and psychotic themes I have traced in this study. The Expressionist violence of *The Ghost Sonata* will in future cast its dark shadow over all single-mindedly lyrical or ineffably Symbolist celebrations of Eliot's hyacinth garden. But it does not in itself compel a reading of those lines in the light of the occluded phantasy of the drowned girl, and such an interpretation can only establish itself compellingly by drawing the rest of the text within its ambit. Eliot's narrator may not face Strindberg's formidable cook, but he does encounter Madame Sosostris, herself a transformation of the Sybil of the epigraph. Just as the cutting of the cards in *Sweeney Agonistes* carries the narrative of Doris's death beyond the abrupt close of the unfinished play, so here too the device tells a murderous tale, though a less one-sided one than Kenner assumes. It may be comforting not to find the Hanged Man, but the Tarot deck lives up to its reputation as a 'wicked pack of cards' by turning up 'your card, the drowned Phoenician sailor' and 'Belladonna, the Lady of the Rocks' (*CP*, p. 64) – pointing forward, that is, to the later narrative of 'Death by Water', which was almost extirpated from the poem by Pound's cutting. In her guise as Sosostris the aged Sybil now rounds upon the jeering Greek boys, and the hyacinth girl bites the back that carries her.

After the return from the garden 'I was neither / Living nor dead'. The protagonist is thus fit company for Sweeney's murderer, who finds that after doing a girl in 'Death is life and life is death', 'You're either or neither' (*CP*, p. 134). Since the latter knew that if he *were* alive then the milkman and rent-collector were not, he too, had he ever stood on London Bridge, might have reflected, 'I had not thought death had undone so many' (*CP*, p. 65). I take it that Eliot's use of Dante here, this transformation of London into the Inferno, denotes the text's crossing of that 'frontier' into a realm where one's acts are eternal that was achieved by murdering a mistress in 'Eeldrop and Appleplex'. Madame Sosostris first foresaw 'crowds of people, walking round in a ring', immediately after her injunction to fear death by water (*CP*, p. 64). This fear, unlike that prompted by the handful of dust, is clearly persecutory: the crowds do not simply image the torpor of modern urban life, but are rather the scattered fragments of the destroyed internal object marshalling its forces to rebound on the aggressor. Towards the end of the poem these crowds become the red sullen faces that sneer and snarl. Their persecutory aspect heightened by the characteristic oral imagery ('mountain mouth of carious teeth' – *CP*, p. 76), they are the forerunners of the Eumenides of *The Family Reunion*.

In 'The Fire Sermon' too the victim retaliates. Set on the banks of the Thames, this section of the poem inevitably approaches the repressed central phantasy, and the last fingers of leaf clutching and sinking into the wet bank obliquely acknowledge the last futile struggles of a drowning hyacinth girl. As he fishes in the dull canal and meditates on his collection of 'bones cast in a little low dry garret' (*CP*, p. 70), the Fisher King has something of the grisly casualness of that other murderer who takes in the milk and pays the rent while his girlfriend soaks in lysol. Killing one's mistress becomes almost routine in Eliot's verse, and the real point is to carry it off with this impressive degree of unruffled aplomb. But the dead object is not long subdued. Fragmented as it inevitably is in destructive phantasies, it recoils upon its aggressor in the accusatory chorus of the Thames daughters. Like the juxtaposition of Bleistein and Canaletto in 'Burbank with a Baedeker', the brisk swell of the Elizabethan river is set against a modern Thames that 'sweats / Oil and tar' (*CP*, p. 73), for the river is endowed with the persecutory horror of its nymphs and becomes a nightmare of heaving slime. The text is only partially successful in confining the 'undoing' of these three women to the sexual, to those minor tribulations of casual fornicating that fit its public theme. The first Thames daughter 'raised [her] knees/Supine on the floor of a narrow canoe' (*CP*, p. 74); but part of the stark and chilling force of this act for Eliot is surely that it is as much the gesture of childbirth as it is of sex. It is this importunate physicality that Eliot will shear away from the 'virgin' mothers of his later verse; and *The Waste Land*, in some obscure process of poetic gestation, delivers at sea the infant textual germ that will ultimately be 'Marina'. Eliot matches this resonant and dangerous female with a note as menacing as she: 'disfecemi Maremma' (*CP*, p. 84), where she was 'pushed out of a castle window on her husband's orders' to her death.[8] The third Thames daughter is victim of some psychotic collapse that may also have less to do with sexual exploitation than it does with 'the broken fingernails of dirty hands', for these fingers, in attempting to 'hold on tight' against physical threat, have momentarily clutched, then sunk (*CP*, pp. 74, 63). These accusing Thames daughters prefigure the more lethal sirens of the manuscript 'Death by Water': deprived by Pound of this proleptic role, they have been as immobilised poetically as the Daphne-figure of his 'The Girl' was physically.

The metamorphosis of victim into aggressor had already been effected in muted form in the myth of Philomel, raped and mutilated by Tereus but returning as a persecutory (though never quite decipherable) voice. It had been fear of the recoil of the dead object that charged with tension that sinister dialogue of murderers that closed 'The Burial of the Dead'. The garden in which the corpse is planted is a locale hardly less intimate than one's bathroom, and that the images of sprouting and blooming now convey paranoid horror is testimony how little secure the reparative impulse of the poem's opening actually was. As ever, a woman runs a terrible risk. In lines that recall the hyacinth episode, the neurasthenic Queen of 'A Game of Chess' asks, 'Do / You know nothing? . . . Are you alive or not?' (*CP*, p. 67), perhaps provoking a fate more serious than checkmate. In the draft her interlocutor murmurs ominously, 'I remember / The hyacinth garden' (*WLF*, p. 19); Eliot's footnote to line 126 still keeps residually alive a connection that was deleted from the final text. The fate of the hyacinth girl is, anyway, re-enacted in this section: if the text cowers before the formidable Cleopatra of its opening lines, it will later have its vengeance by decimating her rank of pawns. With the final quotation – 'Good night . . . sweet ladies' (CP, p. 69) – it transforms them into Ophelias about to plunge to a watery end.

The persecutory crowds and fragments announce the poem's regression into the paranoid–schizoid after the shortlived declarations of the depressive superego. So indeed does the very hermeneutic effort necessary to track the permutations on the central phantasy of the drowned woman; the text never faces its own violence unflinchingly enough to achieve lasting reparation, and there remain troubled areas of itself that it is 'forbidden to see' (*CP*, p. 64). Its projected violence returns unerringly upon itself, however, as was the promise of the first two Tarot cards. Phlebas's fate has too often been regarded as rather enviable, a cool lyric interlude in an otherwise tormented text. But he is the target of prolonged oral attack, though the current that 'Picked his bones in whispers' (*CP*, p. 75) is admittedly an exquisite connoisseur of cannibalistic incorporation, a Jamesian version of Strindberg's grotesque Cook. Eliot's drafts on the drowned Bleistein reveal just how powerfully this phantasy of underwater devouring gripped him (*WLF*, pp. 119–23). The recurrent line from *The Tempest* (Act I, scene ii) has also been deceptive: 'Those were pearls that were his eyes.' Far from denoting a sea-change into something rich and strange, image of the poetic process itself, it rather announces a final fixing into opacity of the human gaze which precludes once and for all the beneficent visual circuit for which Prufrock yearned. It also evokes the unenviable fate of the Bradleyan centre, 'every sphere . . . opaque to the others which surround it' (*CP*, p. 86).

But it is chiefly Pound's ruthless editing that has so obscured the nature of Phlebas's death by water; this section of the poem is now a mere ninth of its original length. Eliot's narrative of a New England fishing-expedition and shipwreck leaves scattered traces all over the body of the poem as presently constituted, but with its suppression they obstinately refuse to cohere. The 'Drifting logs' bobbing on the Thames (*CP*, p. 73) are perhaps the broken timbers of its vessel. The violet hour not only liberates the typist from her desk, but also 'brings the sailor home from sea' (p. 71), and after the claustrophobic amours of the former the text tracks down the latter with notable relief. In the bar in Lower Thames Street are heard the mandoline, the clatter and chatter, 'Where fishmen lounge at noon' (p. 73). By equating the Fisher King with its own New England fisherman, the poem to some extent prises the former loose from all the learned paraphernalia he brings with him from Jessie Weston, moulding him to its own psychic purposes and once more implying that *The Waste Land* is not altogether the lofty cultural diagnosis it would like to take itself to be.

With its haunting vision of the three Sirens singing in the cross-trees of the ship, Eliot's account of the fishing expedition achieves an epiphany every bit as bafflingly intense as that in the hyacinth garden. The blanched trio of weird sisters in the Facsimile will return later in Eliot as the 'three white leopards' of *Ash-Wednesday*, and are related backwards to the singing mermaids 'Combing the white hair of the waves' in 'Prufrock' (*CP*, pp. 97, 17). As they strain forwards from the mast, these Sirens have something of the tense watchfulness we might have expected in the sailor himself, while the lingering rhythms of the latter seem, conversely, to have an unwonted languor. The Sirens' song saps the sailor's professional self-sufficiency, mines his very power of reality-testing, chips bit by bit away at the hypertrophy of depressive separating out for which he had initially been celebrated in a verse form that glances back at the quatrains of *Poems 1920* without, however, fully achieving their taut precision. For it was no accident that the expounder of the 'Impersonal theory of poetry' (*SE*, p. 18) should have chosen to apply that most Eliotic of epithets to his New England sailor. Were this fisherman to turn his hand to verse as well as net-mending between trawls, he would no doubt espouse the unyielding classicism of 'Tradition and the Individual Talent'. Already in this early description the sailor has dissociated the man who suffers from the 'inhuman, clean and dignified' mind that concentratedly ponders nautical chart and sheets (*WLF*, p. 55). The text may wish to claim that even ashore the private man 'retains' a certain professional steeliness, but it cannot convincingly hold the two together; hence its crazy veering of tone from clumsy jocularity (the comedy of his mock gonorrhoea) to the Tennysonian resonances that transfigure this homely New England mariner to the status of Ulysses himself. As a kind of personification of Eliotic theory, the sailor, who will ultimately be destroyed in the manuscript, may hint at the supersession of a poetic of impersonality of which the *public* test of *The Waste Land* will claim, ironically enough, to be the consummate vindication.

Making itself heard above the sound of the wind, the Sirens' eerie song 'charmed my senses'. Its objective value in decibels is, however, notably at odds with its poetic impact; for after the immediately preceding clamour of rending sails and timbers, of screaming breakers, the women's appearance has a curious effect of silence. Their song seems to touch some secret nerve of spirituality in sense itself, even as it simultaneously restores to the creaturely promptings of the senses a will that had inhumanly sheared itself away from them. The song is to a degree a Keatsian 'ditty of no tone', but it also has a more tangible charm in common with the 'pleasant whining of a mandoline' (*CP*, p. 73) in Lower Thames Street; it thus shares the ambivalence of the hyacinth episode, where the language is inextricably erotic and mystical at once. Yet it is the following morning, when the strange music of the Sirens has ended though they may still perch on the ship's mast, that brings the final dangers; for, as Franz Kafka shrewdly observed, 'several have survived the song of the Sirens, but none their silence'.[9] In one sense the women are leading the sailor on to death and he is their hapless victim, but in a poem so dominated by the Grail myth even a humble New England sailor becomes a numinous quester, driving indomitably forward in an effort to wrest a further tune from the women who haunt him.

As next day breaks the ship moves towards an ill-defined white line or wall or barrier at the meeting point of sea and sky. We may interpret this barrier as either the translucent opacity of a gaze that has turned to pearl or as the impenetrable outer skin of a 'finite centre': small wonder, then, in either case, that it provokes the stricken cry of 'Home and Mother'. The ship's movement towards it is no longer a passive scudding before the storm, but rather the result of human agency, an attempt to burst through the barrier into the mutual exchanges of potential space. But that attempt ends in a catastrophic shipwreck which is followed by the description, familiar from the final form of *The Waste Land*, of the drowning Phlebas, who is thus revealed to have been the sailor of the foregoing narrative. As the protagonist lapses into death he invokes an enigmatic '*Another*' (*WLF*, p. 61) whose recognition he seems in some sense to have sought without, however, ever knowing whether it has been conclusively attained. Eliot's '*Another*' is not Dante's, and might rather be set beside Jacques Lacan's capitalised *Autre*: 'the first object of desire is to be recognised by the other'.[10] As Winnicott has argued, this Hegelian recognition is to be sought in the first place in the answering gaze of the mother, without which the individual is trapped in a psychic existence of compliant exteriority, inhuman though clean and dignified. But Phlebas's project to make contact with the Other was never really viable in the narrative. Even before the shipwreck the mother was already split into the familiar imagos: multiple dangerous Sirens, who are later the oral attackers picking the bones, and the idealised maternal landscape, 'Home and Mother'. The momentary jolting recognition that these are not so distinct after all (the menacing presence of the bears in the icescape) is not sustained. Phlebas fails in the Grail quest to restore the Fisher King's fertility, and the two figures, 'not wholly distinct' from each other, slump back into castration. Fixed in 'the rigidity of her own defences' (*PR*, p. 131), appropriating the son as phallus-for-her, the mother subjugates the child to a dual relationship which is not the dialectical interchange of potential space but the extremist world of psychosis.

'What the Thunder Said' labours to return to the work of depressive mourning despite the initial intensification of paranoid terror, the red sullen faces sneering and snarling. Though the 'hooded hordes' still swarm, they are now associated with the 'Murmur of maternal lamentation', evoking guilt as much as fear of retaliation:

> A woman drew her long black hair out tight
> And fiddled whisper music on those strings
> And bats with baby faces in the violet light
> Whistled, and beat their wings
>
> (*CP*, pp. 76–7)

The 'bats with baby faces' are a vivid Kleinian phantasy of the envied riches folded away in the fertile interior of the mother's body. Since Eliot has assured us that 'all the women are one woman' (*CP*, p. 82), and since there is anyway a specific allusion here to Cleopatra brushing her hair out into fiery points, that former scene may now be read in the light of the phantasy articulated in these lines. The 'rich profusion' of the throne-room (*CP*, p. 66), its dense and cloying voluptuousness, is an objectification of the slow viscous inner fermenting of the female body, and even flame, most 'spiritual' of the elments, is clogged and choked, 'fattened' into an obscene corporality of its own. The vials of Cleopatra's perfumes are 'Unstoppered', as if the unmannerly seethings of their contents had elbowed their corks and stoppers aside, and yet the perfumes still 'lurk' within, tenaciously clinging to the internal depths whose thick secretions they are. The bats with baby faces of 'What the Thunder Said' have a more sharply sinister aspect than the earlier luscious scene; they not only testify to the teeming wealth of the maternal body, but also are potential sibling rivals.

They are not, however, the only rivals present in this final section of the poem. In the persistent and disturbing sense of 'the third who walks always beside you' (*CP*, p. 77) there may even be some dim attempt at emerging from the dual relationship into the Oedipal triangle. Under the sway of a new reparative impulse, the text edges closer to its occluded phantasy; the damp gust brings rain and 'Ganga was *sunken*' (*CP*, p. 78; emphasis added), like so many of the poem's women. When the Thunder finally speaks it recalls

> blood shaking my heart
> The awful daring of a moment's surrender
> Which an age of prudence can never retract
> (*CP*, p. 78)

Often taken to refer to the loosing of the self into the exchanges of romantic love, these lines may actually be a little less comfortable than that; there are kinds of vigorous physical exertion other than sex that leave the blood shaking one's heart. This 'moment's surrender' belongs with Kurtzian 'desire, temptation, and surrender' of the poem's original epigraph, which hardly points to a lyrical rendezvous with a hyacinth girl. These lines belong with Eliot's comments on *The Changeling* as referring to that inexorable entrapment in the toils of morality which no amount of subsequent prudence can undo. Or, like 'Eeldrop and Appleplex', they refer to that murderous moment whereby our acts become eternal as we cross the frontier, a grim initiation 'not to be found in our obituaries'.

The Thunder's second intervention re-enacts the draft version of 'Death by Water'. 'Thinking of the key, each confirms the prison' (*CP*, p. 79) in another version of Phlebas's hypertrophied separating out from the object. The 'aethereal rumours' that circulate at nightfall are attenuated echoes of the Sirens' nocturnal music; they revive a 'broken Coriolanus' who could not after all sustain his inhuman, clean and dignified repudiation of his own mother. The text, too, cannot sustain its repressions, and Madame Sosostris's blank card comes as nearly into focus as it ever will:

> *Damyata:* The boat responded
> Gaily, to the hand expert with sail and oar

> The sea was calm, your heart would have responded
> Gaily, when invited, beating obedient
> To controlling hands

The boat has a cheeriness denied to its human occupant(s), and critics disposed to regard the Thunder's speeches as unproblematic guides to moral maturity have been troubled by these lines. Negativity is indeed the keynote of the manuscript deletions here: 'You over on the shore', 'I left without you' and 'Clasping empty hands'. But they were surely excised because they only skirt the issue here. '. . . your heart would have responded/Gaily'; but then why didn't it? If Phlebas sails dolefully away, what exactly has become of his companion? 'The sea was calm': so one could not offer in extenuation of one's guilt at her disappearance the possibility that she was 'swept off deck in the middle of a storm', as is done in *The Family Reunion*. '. . . controlling hands', with its hint of imperiousness, has been too strong meat for the queasy stomachs of moralistic commentators: 'the notion of "controlling" the other person may seem at odds with contemporary ideas of allowing the other complete autonomy'.[11] So it may , but rather more sinisterly it recalls the controlling hands which strangle the lady in 'The Love Song of Saint Sebastian', an exertion that might well leave the blood shaking one's heart. Male hands in *The Waste Land* typically have an expertise and mastery denied to their female counterparts. The house-agent's clerk's 'Exploring hands encounter no defence' from a woman so inert she might as well be dead; later his partner's 'automatic hand' listlessly puts a record on the gramophone (*CP*, p. 72). Similarly, the 'hand expert with sail and oar' in 'What the Thunder Said' (*CP*, p. 79) contrasts with the clutching and sinking fingers, the broken fingernails of dirty hands, elsewhere in the poem.

 A suggestive literary parallel to the Thunder's final speech is Grandcourt's death by drowning while sailing with his wife Gwendolen in *Daniel Deronda* (ch. 56): 'he was turning the sail – there was a gust – he was struck – I know nothing – I only know that I saw my wish outside me'. Like *The Family Reunion*, George Eliot knows that nothing is more traumatic for the subject than when circumstance conspires to actualise his or her projected violence, when the person you ache to shove overboard somehow ends up there anyway. Gwendolen's emotional life is split between her conception of a wholly malicious Grandcourt and an idealised

Deronda, the latter a defence against the murderous impulses
directed at the former; like Middleton's Beatrice, Gwendolen is an
amoral nature caught in the inexorable consequences of her own
acts. Her husband's death remains unresolvable; whether her
hesitation in throwing out a lifeline was significant or a mere
delusion of her disordered thoughts will never be known. Deronda
himself takes a charitable view, but then the text had always shared
its heroine's idealisation of him. The events on Eliot's cheery boat
are also desperately obscure, and my remarks are in the spirit of
'The Dry Salvages': 'hints and guesses,/Hints followed by guesses'
(*CP*, p. 213). None the less, it seems to me that the poem comes
close here to acknowledging its elusive and persistent phantasy of a
drowned woman. If, on the one hand, this is a reparative gesture
(you cannot atone what you have not conceded), it is also, on the
other, the last twist of the poetic knife. Reversing the power
relationships between Gwendolen and Grandcourt, the text
undermines its precursor in good Bloomian fashion, quelling one
insolent heroine as it does so.

The last lines of the poem share this ambivalence. Linguistically it
splinters into a chaos of tongues and citations which are never fully
gathered into the Sanskrit prayer of the last line. 'These fragments I
have shored against my ruins' (*CP*, p. 79), but this makeshift
patching and shoring is a psychic project on a much smaller scale
than the depressive rousings of the cruellest month gave us to
expect; instead of guilt and reparation the poem busily cobbles
together compromise-formations and manic denials against its
psychotic ruins. But this strategy of defence is less purely defensive
than it seems: Hieronymo may be mad again but he contrives to 'fit
you' first. His polyglot drama is an act of vengeance before it is a
work of art, but *The Waste Land* more successfully holds the two
impulses together. It aims to avenge the castrated son even as the
latter seeks violently to wrest the phallus from the mother, and this
primitive Aeschylean drama is overlain by the depressive impulses of
the text's first and last sections. Hence its double bind. The
phantasy of the drowned woman must be self-laceratingly
acknowledged, but at the same time the poem longs to gloat over
and crow about it; the pieces of the maternal body must be lovingly
stitched together even as it yearns to chop them up into still tinier
morsels. Both impulses are imperative and they are ultimately
incompatible; each line and image of *The Waste Land* is bitterly
contested by them. This tension is not, however, sustained in

Eliot's later poetry, where devices of splitting and denial are firmly in command, and it is to these texts that I now briefly turn before discussing Eliot's drama, where the psychic stakes are again much higher.

The Ariel poems of the late 1920s remain listlessly within the pathological version of separating out that is familiar from the full text of 'Death by Water'. An exception here is the much-admired 'Marina'. Exquisitely beautiful as it is, the poem is preceded by an epigraph beside which even Sweeney's tale of the Gopsum Street murder pales. 'What is this place, what country, what region of the world?' cries Hercules as he returns to sanity after having slaughtered wife and children in Seneca's *Hercules Furens*. Periclean recognition and Herculean butchery confront each other to form what Eliot himself described as a 'criss-cross'. But he did not elaborate further, and later critics have been equally reticent, reaching as ever for their Symbolist talismans: 'we can scarcely hope to say what the poem means, only what it is'.[12] So intense is the idealisation of the loved object here that it expels all the violence it aims to deny in the body of the text into its mere outworks or epigraph. This criss-cross effect is probably the most remarkable instance of splitting in all Eliot, yet is not mentioned in the otherwise deeply perceptive account of his poetry by Graham Martin in *Eliot in Perspective*. Martin does not have a Kleinian interest in the theme of 'doing girls in' and construes textual splitting more narrowly than I have done: 'a "splitting" effect [is where] the image keeps some of its early meanings, but sheds others which then re-emerge in different imagistic form'.[13] 'Marina' is a privileged text for this thesis, for it is virtually a compendium of Eliot's recurrent imagery; 'What images return' it coyly admits (*CP*, p. 115). Martin then demonstrates that the laughter that in early Eliot is at once dangerous and 'proto-innocent' is now simply innocent: Mr Apollinax 'laughed like an irresponsible foetus', but 'Marina' records 'Whispers and small laughter between leaves and hurrying feet' (*CP*, pp. 33, 115). The danger, sheared away from these infantile gurglings, reappears in the series of denunciatory images: 'Those who sharpen the tooth of the dog'. Martin also points to a split, prefigured in Tiresias, between physical and spiritual sight; the fog makes the former impossible only to bestow vision on a higher level, 'more distant than stars and nearer than the eye'. Examples might be multiplied. 'The garboard strake leaks, the seams need caulking' (*CP*, p. 116); but of course one needs *pitch* to caulk those leaky seams and, as Jean-Paul Sartre reminds us, 'a slimy substance like pitch is an aberrant fluid'.[14] If slime is the agony of water, water in turn for Eliot contains sliminess within itself as the lurking negation of its own liquidity. In *The Waste Land* the Thames sweats oil and tar, but in 'Marina' sliminess is split so decisively from water that the protagonist's boat is falling apart for want of it. Slime, like physical danger, is displaced to the poem's denunciatory list with its 'sty of contentment' (*CP*, p. 115).

More interesting than successful splitting, however, is its failure, that slow seepage of lethal energies across the binary opposition. With great prescience Graham Martin suggested the ambivalences of sight in 'Marina': the higher vision is precious little help for navigating in fog, and the woodthrush that lures the boat on is bringing 'granite islands towards my timbers' (*CP*, p. 116). The *Waste Land* facsimile has thoroughly confirmed this, and the poem itself seems to be referring to that repressed *Ur*-version as it contemplates the cracked boat: 'I made this, I have forgotten / And remember.' Yet the dilapidated condition of Pericles's boat in this text is a double defence against the memory of the former catastrophe. On the one hand, shipwreck will no longer matter, because the vessel is hardly seaworthy anyway; the granite islands will be something to cling to before the seams finally give way. But the condition of the boat is so wretched that it seems, on the other hand, as if the shipwreck has already taken place elsewhere; the granite rocks and the battered vessel now seem to belong to different story-lines that need not collide. Textual splitting falters, as Martin surmised, but is reinstated at another level. In *Pericles*, as in *The Family Reunion*, a wife is cast overboard, and, while 'Marina' restores the daughter, it maintains a stony silence about her mother.

Ash-Wednesday testifies to the poetic cost of idealisation and splitting. It begins with impulses of guilt and the acknowledgement of an as-yet undefined burden:

> For what is done, not to be done again
> May the judgement not be too heavy upon us
> > (*CP*, p. 96)

But the text is too ready to hand over its psychic energies to the publicly validated rituals and symbolism of Christianity. '. . . what is done' is subsumed within some catch-all notion of original sin, though for a moment it subversively reasserts itself at the poem's close:

> though I do not wish to wish these things
> From the wide window towards the granite shore
> The white sails still fly seaward, seaward flying
>
> (*CP*, p. 104)

The sensuous vigour of these lines belongs less to the seascape in its own right than it does to the text's approach to the invigorating phantasy of the sailing-boats from which women fall and drown. Graham Martin has related the splitting within Eliot's imagery to his religious dualism of a transcendental realm of value and the everyday world of contingency and non-meaning. What seems crucial to me is his Catholic cult of the Virgin Mary, which reproduces on the sexual level the rigid dualism Martin notes: the Blessed Virgin so monopolises female virtue that it becomes almost an act of public hygiene to 'do in' the women one comes across in daily life, necessarily tainted as these latter are. But, if she is a Platonic Form, reducing all imitations to the merest insignificance, she is also a kind of Hegelian *Geist*, existing only in her embodiments. Every woman in some degree incarnates her, and thus she aggravates as well as assuages depressive guilt.

The poem is under the sway of the familiar imagos: an idealised Lady in a white gown is split off from the three white leopards who, as the allusion to Elijah insists, are identified with the persecuting Queen Jezebel. In so far as these leopards are implicitly in the service of the Lady, we might be thought to be encountering an incipient recognition of both Lady and leopards as ambivalent aspects of a *single* object, but this possibility is mooted at the level of content only to be *formally* withdrawn. The lip-smacking complacency with which these beasts seat themselves under the juniper-tree belongs to a vein of zany humour in this passage which consorts uneasily with the hushed intensities of the Lady's meditation. That which had been contained in the bones asks the right questions, but it does so 'chirping', without due sense of the dignity of the occasion, while 'My guts the strings of my eyes and the indigestible portions' have a brute vigour of their own which will not simply proffer itself to oblivion (*CP*, p. 97). When this oral phantasy next breaks through it has less gusto, but still possesses a force that makes its idealised counterpart decidedly thin:

> Damp, jaggèd, like an old man's mouth drivelling, beyond
>   repair,
> Or the toothed gullet of an agèd shark.
>
> (*CP*, p. 99)

When the good imago tries to match this it produces only the routine paradoxes of the second section. The alliterative and rhyming lather into which the poet works himself in section V is effectively dismissed by the brutal final image of 'spitting from the mouth the withered apple-seed' (*CP*, p. 103), and the closing invocation is a last measure of the text's spuriousness:

> Suffer me not to be separated
>
> And let my cry come unto Thee.
> (*CP*, p. 105)

D. W. Harding has described this as 'the cry of the weaned child'.[15] But by compacting these lines together in his own citation, he obscures the fact that the intervening white space gives a clinching cadence to the last line that satisfies its plea even as it makes it; the gap opens up distance only the more consolingly to affirm an intimacy that was anyway guaranteed by syntactic connection. There is no real separation here, and this is the index of a collapse into the sweetness of manic idealisation that only the text's guts and the strings of its eyes have energy enough left to protest about.

In 'Marina' defensive splitting took place between poem and epigraph, and in the late 1930s and early 1940s that split is reproduced within Eliot's literary activity as a whole as he engaged alternately in dramatic and poetic writing. Just as *Burnt Norton* was itself split off from *Murder in the Cathedral*, so *The Family Reunion* stands apart within the chronology of the Quartets themselves: *Burnt Norton* 1935, *The Family Reunion* 1939, *East Coker* 1940, *The Dry Salvages* 1941, *Little Gidding* 1942. This makes *The Family Reunion* more than usually amenable to the Kleinian themes I am pursuing, but *Four Quartets* more than usually intractable. I propose only to point out that the 'still point' (*CP*, p. 191) whose nature and meaning they explore is not unrelated to these issues. That was already suggested in the early poem 'Silence', and is much more evident in 'Coriolan', where the 'still point of the turning world' (*CP*, p. 140) was explicitly related to the hero's repressed yearning to lapse out into maternal protectiveness. *Four Quartets* implies the Symbolist historiography that Eliot sketched in 'The Metaphysical Poets': the still points that fitfully illuminate the contemporary individual's life are the postlapsarian fragments of a unified sensibility that characterised the *social* existence of seventeenth-century England. Theories of 'organic community' seem to involve an historical projection of Winnicott's potential space, and it therefore comes as no surprise to discover Winnicott himself (who knew Eliot's writings well) arguing that the 'intermediate area' between inner and outer realities 'appears in full force in the work characteristic of the so-called metaphysical poets (Donne, etc.)' (*PR*, p. xi). Here, clearly, is an analyst well versed in 'dissociations of sensibility' outside the clinical situation. It is only because Eliot splits off the more fraught aspects of the infant–mother relationship into *The Family Reunion* that he can achieve the equanimity of philosophical and historical exposition that he does in *Four Quartets*, and it is therefore to that play, and his drama generally, that I now turn.

Comparing Wordsworth unfavourably with Coleridge in 1933, Eliot commented that the former 'had no ghastly shadows at his back, no Eumenides to pursue him' (*UPUC*, p. 69). Six years later he was to generate an entire play from that image, for *The Family Reunion* is constructed in continuous and uneasy relationship to Aeschylus's trilogy *Oresteia*, and particularly its final part, *The Eumenides*. But Eliot's fascination with the work long antedated his own play; it had afforded the epigraph to 'Sweeney among the Nightingales' and to *Sweeney Agonistes*, where the dead mistress soaking in lysol is a riposte to the hewing to death of Agamemnon in the first part of Aeschylus's play. An equal devotion to the *Oresteia* was evinced by Melanie Klein, among whose posthumous papers was found a substantial though unfinished interpretation of it. Unlike Winnicott, Klein had probably *not* read Eliot, and this convergence of interest between the two seems to me a telling piece of external confirmation of the deep affinities between their work that I am exploring here.

For Klein the *Oresteia* is the record of a transition from the paranoid–schizoid to the depressive position, a transition which is at once that of Orestes and of the wider society to which he belongs. In the new order installed by Athena this psychic transformation is graphically symbolised by the Erinyes becoming the Eumenides; a primitive, retaliatory superego becomes a depressive one that provokes guilt and the impulse to reparation. This transition is made by Orestes after his murder of his mother Clytemnestra, and this murder is above all an attack on the breast, a point made dramatically when Clytemnestra bares her breast to her son in a last effort to ward off his violence. That she nearly succeeds, that his vengeful purpose momentarily falters, indicates that from the beginning there were strong depressive elements of love and respect for the autonomy of the object in his relationship to the breast. If he escapes from the paranoid–schizoid position, it is because he was never really there in the first place, but only regressed to it after the murder.[16] Yet this psychic transition is yoked by Aeschylus to a second innovation as the Athenian court legislates, at Apollo's prompting and with Athena's casting vote, that murder of a mother is a trifle beside the killing of a husband. 'No mother gave me birth', vaunts Athena,[17] and the new tutelary deities of Athens are as deeply misogynistic as Ezra Pound and T. E. Hulme themselves could have wished. Matriarchy succumbs to patriarchy, the rule of the father is reinstated, and the depressive separating out of Orestes comes to look suspiciously pathological.

Yet for all this Orestes remains the matricidal son in the *Oresteia* in a way that he does not in Sophocles's *Electra*, and brief comparison of these works may be illuminating. In Clytemnestra's nightmare Sophocles has her see Agamemnon return to life, seize the sceptre which 'now Aegisthus carries' and plant it; it grows into a tree (Orestes) which casts a sinister, vengeful shadow over Mycenae. Aeschylus, in contrast, has Clytemnestra dream that she gives birth to a snake which brutally wounds the breast she offers to it. Later Sophocles replaces Aeschylus's confrontation between Orestes and Clytemnestra by the encounter of Orestes with Aegisthus; mention only is made of Orestes's madness after he has killed his mother. The effect of these variations is to reinstate the *father* as central; Orestes becomes primarily the prince who retains his father's throne by expelling its usurpers. Matricide blurs as the play focuses on the murder of Aegisthus, the conflict between son and mother's lover who usurps the paternal sheets as well as throne, and the last word is given to the reaffirmation of Oedipal truth, not altogether surprisingly in the author of *Oedipus Rex*. What is striking in the *Oresteia*, however, is the obliteration of the father until the play's very end. Having hewn him to death in the bath, Clytemnestra becomes the phallic mother and Aegisthus is a shadowy, rather contemptible figure. Even the dream that foretells

Clytemnestra's downfall does not have the triangular structure of the Oedipus complex, but is rather, as André Green has remarked,

> the drama of a corporal return in which part of herself is detached, becomes autonomous and kills her. This part, which is precisely the part desired by herself as a phallic attribute, renders the masculine presence superfluous or anonymous, and implies no reverence for its speech.[18]

The son's task is then to break out of this dual relationship, wresting the phallus away from the mother by his identification with the law of the father; killing the male usurper is a largely derivative task. Backed by Zeus, Apollo and the motherless Athena, Orestes can achieve that identification, and yet in another sense he achieves nothing at all. Fleeing from the phallic mother of Mycenae, he leaps straight into the lap of the phallic goddess of Athens. Aeschylus's text seems to me altogether less orderly than Melanie Klein's neat schematisation would allow, and *The Family Reunion* will tangle its unruly predecessor still further.

Harry Monchensey is an Orestes figure, pursued by the Eumenides and seeking to expiate a murder, but Eliot has curiously compacted past and present of the Aeschylean time-scheme. For a brief moment Harry even appears as the returning Agamemnon: 'Get Downing to draw you a hot bath', counsels Amy (*FR*, p. 30), sinisterly enough in the light of the Atridean commander's fate. The mother's first gesture on the son's return thus re-enacts the founding effacement of the father. Whereas Orestes had the straightforward task of expiating the murder of his mother, Harry has a more paradoxical predicament: he returns to face his mother already having a 'murder' (of his wife) to expiate, and his means of expiation will be, precisely, the murder of his mother. For that he does murder her there can be no doubt. While the text evades by pushing off stage the most intimate encounter of mother and son (it is heralded by Harry's ominous reflection that 'I think, mother, / I shall make you lie down' (*FR*, p. 83) – his first direct speech to her in the play), it allows Dr Warburton to warn Harry of his mother's frailty and the need to protect her from shock. There is a subdued irony in this since the doctor is a shadowy Aegisthus, usurping the father's role by leading Amy into dinner; conducting his own clandestine diagnosis of Harry and leaking the medical information that he believes will bend the son to his mother's will, Warburton unwittingly delivers over the very method of retaliation Harry had previously lacked. Once forewarned, Harry blithely proceeds to give his mother the deepest shock he can by announcing that he intends to leave home at once, and Amy leaves the stage to die. The very moment when Harry effectively 'does in' his mother is also the moment when the Eumenides assume their benign, non-persecutory form. There could hardly be a more startling reversal of the unproblematic psychic maturing that Klein discerned in Aeschylus.

Amy is endowed with all the phallic power of a Clytemnestra, consigning Harry's father to a vague and marginal existence: 'when we would have grasped for him, there was only a vacuum' (*FR*, p. 72). André Green argues that in the *Oresteia* the father is present 'only as an obliterated reference',[19] and this is equally true of *The Family Reunion*, where everything 'has always been referred back to mother' (*FR*, p. 70). Mary may be the equivalent of Aeschylus's Electra, but Eliot's text makes her a mere niece and not daughter of Amy in order that the latter shall have borne nothing but sons – Arthur, John, Harry. For the woman whose function it is to produce only sons is yet another version of the phallic woman. 'I *would* have sons, if I could not have a husband', exclaims Amy (*FR*, p. 109), and the sexual acts in which those sons were conceived have been a vampiric 'forcing' of his seed from an 'unwilling father'. As in Aeschylus, the 'usurper' Warburton is a mere convenient tool in this Clytemnestra's capable hands. It is this dominating mother that Harry must quell, and, if he appears to have made a false start in throwing his wife from the liner, the text swiftly reveals at whom that destructive impulse was actually directed. Far from having resulted, as Amy believes, in a decisive overthrow of her maternal domination, Harry's marriage has in fact only delivered him over to a woman who repeats in essentials the characteristics of that mother. 'She wouldn't leave him alone', elucidates Downing; 'She wouldn't leave him out of her sight' (*FR*, p. 38); and in Amy's own description of Harry's wife there is hardly an epithet that does not glance sideways at her own relationship with her son. Downing, the voice of bluff commonsense, considers the wife's tense watchfulness to be neurotically unreasonable; but in a poetic *oeuvre* where the woman runs a terrible risk it seems to me simply prudent to keep one's marital relations on a permanent alert. The dangerous moments are when you 'lean over a rail' (*FR*, p. 38), averting your vigilant gaze. We need not altogether endorse the text's judgement of Harry's wife, just as, I shall argue later, there are grounds for resisting its view of Amy.

But Harry's phantasy of pushing his wife from the ship remains, none the less, a phantasy attack on the mother. Whether he actually pushed her remains obscure. As far as the text is officially concerned he of course did not, but it leaves tantalisingly open, by means of minor narrative discrepancies, the possibility that he did. The newspapers reported that she was 'Swept off the deck in the middle of a storm' (*FR*, p. 19); but Harry, like Charles Baudelaire, is capable of a damnation denied to newspaper editors. Downing 'took a bit of air before [he] went to bed' (*FR*, p. 38), which, in one so commonsensical, is an odd thing to do in the middle of a storm. The less balanced Harry manages to remain 'Leaning over the rail, looking at the water' (*FR*, p. 39) for a full half-hour while Downing strolls about, and if his wife was swept away it is difficult to understand how he, in this precarious position, was not. Earlier Harry has spoken of 'that *cloudless* night in the mid-Atlantic' (*FR*, p. 28; emphasis added). Determined that 'I only dreamt I pushed her' (*FR*, p. 97), the text sports secretly with the other option, and this is just one local example of its flair for having its psychic cake and eating it.

Even if it is only phantasised, however, the 'push' remains traumatic, leading to retaliatory persecution by the Eumenides, because the contingent *fact* of Harry's wife having been simultaneously swept overboard leads to a revival of infantile omnipotence, as if the mere wish were – magically and instantaneously – the deed itself. There is a breakdown of reality-testing; it appears that the real object has not survived a mere phantasy attack; like Gwendolen Harleth, Harry suddenly sees his wish outside him. By displacing Harry's aggression from mother to mother surrogate and by embodying it in a narrative of a woman falling / being pushed from a boat, Eliot brings this play into close relation to *The Waste Land* and provides retrospective confirmation of my argument about the central phantasy of that poem. If Harry is indeed to achieve a depressive resolution of his paranoid terrors, he will have to acknowledge that his violence has bearing not on his wife but on his mother. The play wants both to claim that he does, and yet to cushion him from the full pain of that recognition. It will do so by providing him with an idealised mother and a dead father onto whom his violence towards the real mother can be safely projected.

Harry and Agatha share a fine scorn for those whose attention is directed to the superficial level of events and actions; the contemptible gaggle of uncles and aunts are capable of grasping 'only events: not what has happened' (*FR*, p. 26). They do their best to deflect critical attention away from the play's climactic moment, which is itself an 'event' and not one of their interminable explanations. After Agatha has allowed Harry to reconstruct his family past, there follow the stage directions, '*The* EUMENIDES *appear ... The curtains close.* AGATHA *goes to the window, in a somnambular fashion, and opens the curtains, disclosing the empty embrasure. She steps into the place which the* EUMENIDES *had occupied* (*FR*, p. 102). More eloquent than the dense passages of verse that purport to motivate it, this emblematic action may be illuminatingly compared with Melanie Klein's account of the painter Ruth Kjar.[20] Once a decorative painting had been removed from the wall of Kjar's room she suffered an intense depression; the empty space 'grinned hideously down at her'. Not until she began a life-size painting of a naked negress to fill the space did the depression clear, and thus began her career as a painter. Klein relates the initial crisis to the destruction of the internal mother and subsequent inner void, which were resolved by the symbolic re-creation of the good internal object in her own painting. The relevance of this to *The Family Reunion* may now be clear. Harry's first glimpse of his mother as he returns from his eight-year absence is framed by a window; arriving at dusk he sees his mother in the lighted drawing-room. But, if Amy formidably fills the frame, it by the same token constricts and contains her; she may be an alarming apparition to her returning prodigal, but she is at the same time unknowingly subjected to his sinister gaze: 'Do you like to be stared at by eyes through a window?' (*FR*, p. 23). His confession of the 'murder' is then a reliving of the phantasy attack on the mother which destroys the good object in the frame. But, unlike Ruth Kjar, Harry does not have a depressive sense of blank space, because his aggression returns upon himself in the paranoid form of the Eumenides, who occupy the window during his conversation with Mary. It is not until Agatha herself enters the frame that Harry has restored an image of the mother; it is neither the real mother nor a symbolic recreation of her, but rather an idealised substitute. The real mother can now be destroyed because the idealisation allows a manic denial of aggression.

This strategy is reinforced by Harry's quest for and recovery of his dead father, a curiously Sophoclean interlude in this otherwise Aeschylean text. André Green has pointed out that, whereas 'the *Oedipodeia* unfolds like an attempt to interpret a forgotten dream, in which each stage by which it is elucidated helps us also to recall it', the *Oresteia* 'unfolds in the dimension of the dream itself, as the action actually takes place'.[21] One strand of *The Family Reunion* is precisely the attempt to recover a buried past. 'I always said his Lordship / Suffered from what they call a kind of repression', remarks Downing (*FR*, p. 37), though his dismissiveness ('what they call') implies that this psychoanalytical vocabulary does not really have a purchase here. But there is a repression notwithstanding, and it first begins to lift in conversation with Mary as Harry confronts the blank unhappiness of their childhood. But the crucial return of the repressed occurs in his encounter with Agatha that immediately precedes her occupation of the embrasure. She reveals that, as a consequence of her affair with him, Harry's father concocted 'a dozen foolish ways' to kill Amy (*FR*, p. 96); while she had no general objection to that purpose, she prevented him because Amy was at that time pregnant with Harry. Having saved the foetus's life, Agatha now claims a maternal right to it – 'I felt that you were in some way mine' (*FR*, p. 97) – and this dubious logic facilitates Harry's own substitution of her for his real mother. Like her holy predecessor in *Ash-Wednesday*, Agatha too has achieved the difficult feat of virgin birth; she is thus lifted clear away from the messy, viscous physicality that Eliot usually associates with women into some realm of unencumbered spirituality, a point reinforced by her spinsterly academic existence as head of a Cambridge college.

Harry is deeply impressed by her news of his father, and, since Eliot's plays often attribute a mystical, self-sufficient value to paternity, it is salutary to bear in mind Klein's reminder that, if the infant values the father's penis, he or she does so chiefly for its strategic usefulness (to administer pleasure or pain) in the more fundamental relation to the mother. So it is here. Harry does not accede to the paternal reference, does not discover the father as an agent of prohibition, a third term violently intervening into the dual relation with the mother. Instead he finds a father in his own image, no less full of murderous intent towards Amy, and this, the text assures us, is the moment of liberation:

Perhaps my life has only been a dream
Dreamt through me by the minds of others. Perhaps
I only dreamt I pushed her.

(*FR*, p. 97)

This is the logic of Eliot's 'Tradition and the Individual Talent'. Unexamined, the past perpetuates itself; understand it, and it becomes a vehicle of liberation. It is also the logic of Freud's 'compulsion to repeat', though stretched over generations rather than confined to a single life: Harry is 'obliged to *repeat* the repressed material as a contemporary experience instead of, as the physician would prefer to see, *remembering* it as something belonging to the past'.[22] Once Harry perceives his murderous wish as only the latest instalment of the family curse, he is free, and the play might aptly be retitled 'Tradition and the Individual Death-Wish'. But free of what, precisely? Merely the illusion that he pushed his wife? But murder of the wife was never really at issue in the first place, for the text pointedly presents Harry's wife as a mother surrogate for him; it is offering us a logic here that it itself does not believe in. Freedom for Harry could only be a matter of acknowledging violence towards the mother, but he does not do so, and the play itself is still more evasive, chorically attributing the disaster to 'certain inflexible laws / Unalterable' (*FR*, p. 91). The text exculpates Harry with one hand even as it reveals how far-reaching his destructiveness is with the other. Unless we are to regard the car smashes in which his two brothers are involved as meaningless stage bustle, giving an illusion of plot and activity as do the lost spectacles and the bungled cooking of *The Cocktail Party*, then they too must be interpreted as further evidence of Harry's hostility. In Kleinian terms, he seeks to destroy not only the maternal body itself, but also the phantasised riches it contains. Harry's acid comments on his brother John's crash, which so outrage his uncles and aunts, are in turn to be understood in the light of this unconscious aggression.

The Family Reunion does its best to buttress its hero against these accusations: first by making the accusers despicably small-minded, and secondly by granting to Harry and especially Agatha a position of absolute authority whose sanction is ultimately religious. How successful in cowing dissent these devices are may be seen from D. W. Harding's dismissal of concern with Harry's astonishing lack of compunction as 'hopelessly banal and sentimental'.[23] But for a brief moment the prattling aunts had assumed the mantle of genuinely reparative Eumenides. But a more general issue arises here: how is one to comment on a play that so flaunts its own irreducibility? Both Harry and Agatha tirelessly assert that 'You will understand less after I have explained it', or 'In this world / It is inexplicable, the resolution is in another' (*FR*, pp. 26, 111). Good Symbolists that they are, they remorselessly denounce the heresy of paraphrase. But surely the text doth protest too much, attempting to browbeat its audience into the same position of hapless ignorance as the uncles and aunts. A crucial critical question will be how far and effectively it interrogates these lofty affirmations of gnomic superiority, in which it has at the same time a large investment, and whether it will finally allow its paranoid–schizoid phantasies all the authority of the divine order of things itself. A certain unease is generated by Mary's comments to Harry: 'You attach yourself to loathing / As others do to loving' she remarks sharply (*FR*, p. 54), and Agatha will later concur with this perceptive diagnosis. At the same time, however, Mary is the equivalent of Aeschylus's Electra and aligned with Agatha against Amy, an alliance symbolised by their final procession together round the dead mother's birthday cake; Mary's challenge to the Harry–Agatha axis is therefore only momentary, and she is bought off with the hint of a college fellowship. A more sustained assault comes later. 'I wish nothing', claims Agatha as Harry prepares to leave, 'I only say what I know will happen' – to which comes Amy's barbed retort, 'You only say what you intended to happen' (*FR*, p. 104). In this encounter between Amy and Agatha, real mother and idealised substitute, the paranoid viewpoint that the play offers as final wisdom is subverted even as it is expounded, as Eliot himself realised twelve years later when he referred to Amy as 'the only complete human being in the play' and his hero as 'an insufferable prig' (*OPP*, p. 84).

Implicated in the game from the beginning as mistress of Harry's father, there is no position from which Agatha could suddenly claim a transcendental authority; Amy articulates a challenge that she simply cannot meet. This does not exculpate Amy, who remains as passionately self-interested as ever, but her forthright anger none the less shows up as arrogant evasions the cryptic formulations in which Agatha wraps and depersonalises her own self-interest. Like her intellectual sister, Amy too is cut away from that rich biological life that so often characterises Eliot's women and which only emerges here in 'The noxious smell untraceable in

the drains' (*FR*, p. 27) of Harry's lurid visions: purged, in a way to
which Graham Martin has alerted us, of their carnal fascination,
smell and sliminess become merely nauseating in *The Family
Reunion*. It is not her biology but her imperious *will* that
distinguishes Amy; she has more in common with the loftily self-
possessed heroine of 'Conversation Galante' than she does with the
rippling female gullet of 'Hysteria'. That former text is an
illuminating parallel here. Amy's curt abrasiveness cuts through the
turgid periods of her sister in much the way that the laconic
utterances of the lady confute at a stroke the Laforguian
whimsicality in the 'Conversation'. Both the latter discourses claim
to be transparent to truth: Laforguian banter is supply expressive of
the narrator's exquisite sensibility, while Agatha's verse is charged
with the more sombre resonance of 'inflexible laws / Unalterable'
(*FR*, p. 91). Both accuse their adversary of mere obtuseness, yet in
the light of that adversary come to look remarkably uncouth
themselves. Badinage becomes babble, a compulsive dance of
signifiers that halts only at the risk of exposing its 'own vacuity'
(*CP*, p. 35); and when Harry refers obscurely to 'the noise of
machinery' the phrase might be regarded as pointing to the
whirring and clanking labour of production of his aunt's verse (*FR*,
p. 101). But these two linguistic deflations work in opposite
directions. Laforguian subjectivity turns out to be the incidental
effect of a self-generating *écriture*, while the unbending
impersonality of Agatha's style is the ploy of a furtively scheming
subject. No wonder, then, that *The Family Reunion* refuses to show
on stage the encounter of mother and son: if Amy could undo the
self-assured Agatha, her dialogue with Harry might have brought
about a *débâcle* much more traumatic than that recorded in
'Conversation Galante'. Harry returns announcing 'Mother is
asleep' (*FR,* p. 85), and in one sense this is vaguely sinister,
anticipating her imminent death as her once superb will fails to
master her physical frailty. But, at the same time, her 'insufferable
prig' of a son just *is* extremely soporific.

The contradictions of Agatha's position emerge by contrast with
the play's Aeschylean sources. Agatha is at once Cassandra and
Athena. Like the former she is a prophetess who has deflected the
father's affections away from the text's Clytemnestra, and like the
latter she is the presiding genius of the final restoration of order.
But, since she takes Amy's son away from her, directing him to a
fate that undoubtedly leads to death, she reveals more strikingly still

Eliot's tangled adaptation of his source. *The Family Reunion* ends where the *Oresteia* began, with the abducting of a child from its mother and its subsequent sacrifice; Harry and Agatha are now seen to be re-enacting the roles of Iphigenia and Agamemnon. Though she has the best of their linguistic exchanges, Amy can hardly hope to overcome a foe as formidable as this, particularly as the latter is backed by a set of Eumenides who have become Eliotic sirens: 'Now I see at last that I am following you', cries Harry (*FR*, p. 102). Eliot's text thus unpicks and restitches its predecessor to create a murderous constellation in Agatha – Cassandra, Athena and Agamemnon rolled into one. The play ends with the procession round the birthday cake which is its grim parody of the libation-bearing in Aeschylus. Whereas there the scene was a reverent offering of nourishment to the dead father, here it announces a sadistic devouring of the dead mother. But this is an attack that is also an incorporation, as the mother is forcibly compelled to yield the living substance she denied in life; in this sense, as we shall see, *The Family Reunion* might be regarded as an answer to 'Gerontion'.

The play destroys Amy, but does not escape her. It remains 'persecuted' by the possibility of a reading that has taken the weight of her case against Agatha, and its author too joined the Erinyes in 'Poetry and Drama'. Those 'indigestible portions' which resisted the idealisation of *Ash-Wednesday* (*CP*, p. 97) are reassembled into the 'complete human being' that is Amy (*OPP*, p. 84) only to be parcelled anew with the birthday cake of the play's close; and it is now a feminist criticism, Kleinian or otherwise, that must resume the depressive work.

In Eliot's subsequent plays the tension has dropped. Though that is not without its advantages (there is less of the self-preening obscurity that characterises the verse of *The Family Reunion*), it also marks a withdrawal from the radical explorations of that earlier play. So thorough-going are the defences of *The Cocktail Party* that there is little hint of depressive pain. The play itself attempts to rule out a psychoanalytical interpretation by having Reilly, who is both psychotherapist and religious director, dismiss psychoanalysis as mere buttress of the patient's vanity. But the success of its major strategy is shown by D. W. Harding's bafflement with 'Reilly's account of his original intuition (expressed in an apparition) that Celia was destined to die a violent death. It seems beside the point: the significance of her choice was unconnected with the variety of death to which she was on her way.'[24] The violent death of a woman is not simply *to* the point in Eliot; it usually *is* the point. In *The Family Reunion* Amy was an obstinate manipulator of men, a quality for which she was to die of a violent shock from her son. Though the parent–child relationship is apparently not at issue in *The Cocktail Party*, the play none the less preserves those two features of Amy, splitting them between Celia (violent death) and Lavinia (domination of Edward). Eliot's first account of Celia's martyrdom by crucifixion beside an ant-hill was so gruesome that it had to be toned down in performance, a detail that shows emotional forces at work stronger than the play as it now stands can support. At a deep structural level *The Cocktail Party* works essentially the same material as its predecessor and grants itself the same paranoid–schizoid satisfaction: the omnipotent destruction of a maternal object that is conceived as aggressive and threatening. But in another sense the mother has the last word after all. 'Harry is going away – to become a missionary', announces Amy with fine sarcasm, though her hapless son complains that 'I never said that I was going to be a missionary' (*FR*, pp. 115–16). The resonance of Celia in the later play is the result of this dual perspective on her: as crucified missionary she is the mother destroyed and avenged in a single textual gesture.

In *The Confidential Clerk* the theme of paternity is predominant, but less for its own sake even now than for its strategic value in repudiating the mother. 'You have no preference? Between a father or a mother?' Mrs Guzzard asks Colby; 'Let my mother rest in peace', comes the curt reply.[25] In fact, of course, there is little need for Colby to repudiate his mother, because he has effectively never had one. The play therefore fails to engage Eliot's deepest preoccupations and is a drearily academic exercise. This is particularly disappointing in view of the fact that Mrs Guzzard, in condensing into her surname both 'guzzle' and 'gizzard', seems unusually well qualified to arouse Eliot's alarm. Its successor, *The Elder Statesman*, is a more moving piece in its return to the concerns of *The Family Reunion*. Lord Claverton is burdened with a sense of futility because he has suppressed the memories of his guilty involvement in his youth with Gomez and Mrs Carghill. Two distinct but complementary images from the past recur in the course of the play: a midnight drive in which Claverton ran over an old man in the middle of the road but refused to stop, and a day's punting in Oxford with Mrs Carghill and two other girls. Undo the work of splitting, condense the two images, bringing the violence of the one into relation with the narrative situation of the other, and the central phantasy of both *The Waste Land* and *The Family Reunion* stands forth: the violent death of a woman on or from a boat. This, then, is what Claverton has never acknowledged, remaining instead subject to the persecutions of a paranoid superego:

> What is this self inside us, this silent observer,
> Severe and speechless critic, who can terrorise us
> And urge us on to futile activity,
> And in the end, judge us still more severely
> For the errors into which his own reproaches drove us?[26]

This superego is objectified in the conspiratorial return of Gomez and Mrs Carghill, whom Claverton himself recognises as 'merely ghosts:/Spectres from my past' (p. 56). But they are not only persecuting Eumenides, for Gomez demands recognition as well as revenge, just as Claverton's response to them is not only paranoid: he fears retaliation, but also says of Mrs Carghill that 'we should respect love always when we meet it . . . we must not abuse it' (p. 58). There is thus in the play an unusually strong depressive and reparative component. Since one of the main themes is the relationship between father and daughter, *The Elder Statesman* recalls 'Marina', but, whereas the poem used an intense idealisation of the daughter to expel aggression outside the text into the epigraph, Claverton abandons the omnipotent idealisation of his own daughter and accepts her autonomy. This creates a beneficent potential space between self and object in which the phantasy of aggression can at last be acknowledged. Monica's final invocation of 'the certainty of love unchanging' (p. 70) rivals the lofty pitch of many of Harry and Agatha's speeches, but is wholly without the merely intimidating afflatus with which Eliot had attempted to ward off depressive pain and insight in *The Family Reunion*. The conclusion of *The Elder Statesman* is not wholly secure; there is, for example, a residual attempt to deny violence by contriving that the pedestrian Claverton ran down was already dead. But it comes as near as any Eliot text ever does to bearing the psychic consequences of Sweeney's claim that any man has to, needs to, wants to, once in a lifetime (if not a good deal more often), do a girl in.

5 Stiffening in Conclusion: 'Gerontion' and the 'Objective Correlative'

Though written immediately after the quatrain poems, 'Gerontion' breaks loose from the formal constraints of its predecessors to explore what Empson has termed the 'echoes and recesses of words'.[1] But if in this sense the text is courageously open to experience, the self-dramatisation it effects by its Jacobean rhetoric insulates it at the same time. Gerontion may be at the mercy of his own connotations, but he is also covertly 'cheering himself up' in ways that were familiar to Eliot as a critic of *Othello*: 'Othello succeeds in turning himself into a pathetic figure, by adopting an *aesthetic* rather than a moral attitude, dramatising himself against his environment' (*SE*, pp. 130–1). This is not quite Eliot's own way of consoling himself: more ambitious than Othello, he will settle for nothing less than the wholescale incorporation of his environment. This desire to 'see one's wish outside one' involves submitting the map of contemporary Europe to the contours of one's own psyche, but this is not, needless to say, the way Eliot himself sees the process. In 'Tradition and the Individual Talent' he argues that, if the poet has acquired enough erudition, has extinguished self before the austere monuments of the Tradition, then what he will dredge up will no longer be the Kleinian octopuses and angels, but rather the 'mind of Europe' (*SE*, p. 16). What requires pointing out here is just how often the morsels of the European mind that surface have to do, in one way or another, with the general theme of doing girls in. Erudition supposedly saves one from the tawdriness of mere 'personality', but Gerontion himself knows that a citation may also be a 'concitation'. The lofty monuments have an uncanny knack of reflecting back those intimate phantasies they were intended to chasten; it is no accident that the very doctrine of 'cheering oneself up' is articulated as Eliot contemplates Othello's last major speech after murdering Desdemona. In his essay on Thomas Middleton, one of the major statements of 'impersonality', Eliot remarks that the dramatist 'has no message; he is merely a great recorder': 'his greatness is not that of a peculiar personality, but of a great artist or artisan of the Elizabethan epoch' (*SE*, pp. 169, 162). Yet his account of Middleton's achievement is all octopuses and angels. On the one hand, there is the murderous heroine of *The Changeling*, 'moral only by becoming damned', and, on the other, the 'Roaring Girl': 'a type of the sort of woman who has renounced all happiness for herself and who lives only for a principle . . . a free and noble womanhood' (*SE*, p. 170). The mind of England and Europe may itself be afflicted by Kleinian phantasies, and it is accordingly necessary to pick one's way suspiciously through the learned paraphernalia that clutters 'Gerontion'.

Waiting, like its protagonist, 'for rain', 'Gerontion' is surely Eliot's most desiccated text: 'Rocks, moss, stonecrop, iron, merds' (*CP*, p. 39). In 'stonecrop' even vegetation becomes little more than a mineral excrescence of the unyielding soil it subsists on, and in 'merds' the faeces lose the moist fascination they so often have in Eliot. The French neologism stuns the physical substance itself, but this is not only the poet's fastidious distancing of himself from taboo libidinal pleasures; more radically, there is some essential impoverishment in the faeces, a congealing into the brute materiality of rocks or iron. Nothing could be further removed from the 'liquid siftings' of 'Sweeney among the Nightingales' (*CP*, p. 60). Yet this bitter impoverishment was always latent in Eliotic excrement and entails the splitting apart of a profound ambivalence.

In *The Waste Land* Facsimile Fresca had 'slipped softly' to the needful stool, where she whiled away her time reading Samuel Richardson (*WLF*, p. 23), and her momentary reappearance in line 67 of 'Gerontion' confirms her relevance to the theme of 'merds'. Eliot's description of Fresca affords an instance of the rhetorical figure of hypallage, that transposition of the natural relations of two elements in a proposition which may itself be regarded as a form of Kleinian splitting. 'Gerontion' contains a minor example: the woman is 'poking the peevish gutter' (*CP*, p. 39). Her rebellious irritation (she 'keeps' – both defends and is confined to – the kitchen) is thus defused by its rhetorical displacement onto the gutter itself. In the Fresca passage the physical qualities of the faeces themselves slip softly across the line to adhere to the description of her physical movement. But at the same time the process of excretion is explicitly a labour, a hard and bitter one indeed if she needs a novel as long as Richardson's to occupy her. Moist and solid at once, eager for escape yet obstinately clinging, the faeces share the ambivalence of *The Waste Land*'s unguent perfumes, 'unstoppered' and 'lurking' at the same time (*CP*, p. 66). They can neither be securely stowed away within the intimate cavities of the subject's body, nor discarded safely as mere waste products into the public realm. If Fresca returns to bed in the Facsimile thinking that she has disposed of the faeces, she is soon proved wrong: some forty lines later every dog in town will 'dung' her.

In 'Gerontion', however, excrement is merely dry inert pats of dung scattered across a stony field. To some degree this is a result of defensive splitting, enacted in the poem in its dealings with the squatting Jew. This latter first has all the mucous stickiness of frogspawn, but is then systematically 'blistered' and 'peeled' as the poem scorches him dry (*CP*, p. 39). But at the same time this desiccation is unwilled and bitterly lamented; Gerontion longs for nothing more than the chance to wallow in a mud bath, 'knee deep in the salt marsh, heaving a cutlass'. 'I have lost my sight, smell, hearing, taste and touch', he cries (*CP*, p. 41), and what he yearns for is a Sartrean viscosity that would nourish these senses. The 'caressing hands' of Mr Silvero and Fräulein von Kulp's 'one hand on the door' (*CP*, pp. 39, 40) are dystopian tactile images, each the obverse of the other: the first is a delicately spiritualised play across the mere surfaces and textures of things, while the latter is simply inert, resting leadenly on its object. Gerontion himself dreams of a resistant but not unyielding sliminess in which even so light and swashbuckling a weapon as a cutlass would need to be 'heaved'. It is thus less a case of textual splitting and more of the failure of some inner principle of moistness in the slimy itself that leaves the poem with the unrewarding 'merds' of line 12.

Gerontion himself is inclined to outface this grievous loss:

I have lost my passion: why should I need to keep it
Since what is kept must be adulterated?

(*CP*, p. 41)

Embedded in a pastiche of *The Changeling*, these lines are brought into relation with the final severance of parent and child. Beatrice was taken from her father's blood, but it is in connection with a woman that the adulteration of passion, a disillusionment that reverberates throughout Gerontion's life, is mooted. Since the mind of Europe so often turns out to be a Kleinian octopus, we may set aside the text's portentous references to 'History' and contemporary corridors of power. This is by now a familiar critical move, accompanied by allusions to 'immemorial harlots' (Hugh Kenner) and a deft turning of semantic stones to reveal the sexual undersides of a series of key terms: 'knowledge', 'passages', 'Stiffen', 'rented house', 'shuddering' (*CP*, pp. 40–1).[2] The crux in such interpretations is the second sentence beginning 'Think now':

> She gives when our attention is distracted
> And what she gives, gives with such supple confusions
> That the giving famishes the craving. Gives too late
> What's not believed in, or if still believed,
> In memory only, reconsidered passion. Gives too soon
> Into weak hands, what's thought can be dispensed with
> Till the refusal propagates a fear.
>
> (*CP*, p. 40)

The 'cunning passages', as Hugh Kenner surmises, are indeed those of the female body, but their cunning is less that of sexual coquettishness and more a matter of the furtive biological purposes they pursue. It seems to me that the text evokes here a series of frustrations in the subject–object identity that Winnicott sees as the result of a successful interaction at the maternal breast. If those frustrations repeat themselves in adult sexual life (Kenner's Cleopatra), it is because these relationships are themselves still under the sway of unconscious identifications of the sexual object with the mother. The mother's milk has a certain *a priori* claim to consideration here, because it is one of the few substances which can satisfy the text's clamorous oral demands and restore a lost viscosity; as Roland Barthes writes, 'in the basic morphology of substances milk is the opposite of fire by all the denseness of its molecules, by the creamy, and therefore soothing, nature of its spreading'.[3]

But 'she gives when our attention is distracted'. '. . . attention' I take to be the ego's nascent need for a non-instinctual relation to the breast, 'distracted' here by the very intensity of instinctual demand that has built up. A biological 'craving' is satisfied even as the distinctively human need is 'famished'; response to the breast has only been possible in what Winnicott terms the mode of 'object use' rather than 'object relating'. Or the mother 'gives too late / What's not believed in', and again Winnicott is illuminating. 'The imago in the inner world is kept alive, through the availability of the external separated-off and actual mother, along with her technique of child care, (*PR*, p. 114); but in the case of the mother's absence that reassuring imago can only be cathected for a finite length of time. Should the mother remain away for more than that period, 'then the imago fades, and along with this the baby's capacity to use the symbol of the union ceases'. Nor does the actual mother's belated return mend matters:

> the baby has become *traumatised* . . . has experienced a break in life's continuity, so that primitive defences now become organised to defend against a repetition of 'unthinkable anxiety' or a return to the acute confusional state that belongs to disintegration of nascent ego structure.   (p. 114)

The actual breast may be recalled, but the imago is no longer 'believed' or cathected; there is only a psychotic absence in which it does not exist. The comings and goings of a prematurely autonomous object, product of too brutal a disillusionment of primitive omnipotence, are registered in conscious memory only. Unconscious continuity of the imago is lost: 'after "recovery" . . . a baby has to start again permanently deprived of the root which could provide continuity with the personal beginning' (*PR*, p. 115). Schizoid defences are now organised to counter the baffling unpredictability of a maternal breast which

> Gives too soon
> Into weak hands, what's thought can be dispensed with
> Till the refusal propagates a fear.
>
> (*CP*, p. 40)

'. . . what's thought can be dispensed with' suggests an annihilating phantasy attack such that the reappearance of the actual object, flouting the subject's omnipotence by returning 'too soon', is experienced as a persecutory attack; omnipotent refusal of the breast's existence thus propagates a paranoid fear. After such spectacularly incompetent nursing Gerontion may well ask, 'what forgiveness?' He recalls Eliot's description of Edgar Allen Poe as 'a man of very exceptional mind and sensibility, whose emotional development has been in some respect arrested at an early age' (*CC*, p. 35). Since the psychotic blank of the abandoned imago is crucial in 'Gerontion', it is appropriate that the supple and confusing woman of its central passage should accord with Eliot's account of the absent centre of Poe's verse: 'the ladies in his poems and tales are always ladies lost, or ladies vanishing before they can be embraced' (*CC*, p. 35).

The test of this psychoanalytic hypothesis must lie in its power or lack of it to draw the rest of the poem centripetally about it. Prompted by Winnicott's remark that discussion of the paradoxes of the potential space 'takes special shape in the eternal controversy over transubstantiation' (*PR*, p. xi), it may become clear why the text's invocation of a helpless infantile saviour is immediately succeeded by the predatory leap of 'Christ the tiger':

> In the juvescence of the year
> Came Christ the tiger
>
> In depraved May, dogwood and chestnut, flowering judas,
> To be eaten, to be divided, to be drunk
> Among whispers . . .
>
> (*CP*, p. 39)

Christ is, on the one hand, the idealised mother, offering his living substance for the believer's consumption as unmisgivingly as the perfect mother her milk, and the 'Swaddled' infant the text has just evoked is snugly gratified to the point of stifling. But, on the other hand, this is a parody Eucharist, a satanic ritual enacting a sadistic oral attack on its object and prompting subsequent retaliation: 'The tiger springs in the new year. Us he devours.' It has never quite been explained why Eliot wrote 'juvescence' for 'juvenescence'; his word contains a gap as baffling as the absence that structures Gerontion's entire life. The Eucharist is 'to be divided', a phrase that rings sinisterly; if psychic omnipotence is overthrown by a giving that is too late or that fails in its aim because attention is distracted, it is no less menaced by the knowledge that the precious source of sustenance is also intended for others. Gerontion's contemporaries have now become sibling rivals, and it is no surprise to find them, forty lines later, victims of a phantasy of fierce dismemberment and expulsion. Whirled beyond the circuit of the Bear 'In fractured atoms' (*CP*, p. 41), De Bailhache, Fresca and Mrs Cammel undergo a cosmic version of the car-crashes of Harry Monchensey's brothers.

'Signs are taken for wonders', remarks Gerontion scornfully (*CP*, p. 39), drawing an arcane distinction that has yet to be adequately expounded. In this Eucharistic context it may be useful to juxtapose Gerontion's sign/wonder dichotomy with the more celebrated dualism of allegory and symbol. For either the wine and wafer are mere conventional signs translating abstract notions into picture language, insubstantial tokens to be mechanically decoded step by step, or, as in the Catholic doctrine of transubstantiation, they are symbols, ontologically replete as they magically abolish the gap between signifier and signified. Symbols are the equivalent at the level of language of Gerontion's Utopian substance. Slime may be the agony of water, but 'wonders' are the carnal complacency of signs, fleshing out the fleeting intangibility of the latter with their own plump materiality. But, if from one viewpoint signs are the merest abstractions, ghosts long since separated from their machines, from another they have a turgid inertia and are simply brute chunks of facticity hooked artificially to remote meanings. This unhappy fate too the symbol avoids, its desirable plumpness never becoming an uncouth obesity. Corporeal it may be, but it is illumined by its signified in every particle. Resistant but not impenetrable, flexible but not glibly fleeting, the symbol or 'wonder' offers in linguistic form all the delights of that lost physical sliminess that Gerontion laments.

'Signs are *taken for* wonders' (emphasis added): they are either ignorantly mistaken for their betters or grudgingly accepted as an unavoidable second best. Either way, Gerontion's curt formulation implies that he will settle for nothing less than the real thing. The language of the poem seems to bear him out only to betray him on closer inspection. It initially seems viscous enough, 'swaddling' each signifier in a friendly host of connotations; but the latter achieve an autonomous vitality that hollows out the text on the page, leaving the mere 'echoes and recesses' of words. Later Gerontion abandons his own proud claim:

> These with a thousand small deliberations
> Protract the profit of their chilled delirium,

Excite the membrane, when the sense has cooled,
With pungent sauces, multiply variety
In a wilderness of mirrors.

(*CP*, p. 41)

Both sauce and connotations have transgressed their supplementary role as relishes to become the main course itself, and Eliot is no doubt enjoying an additional pun here at the critic's expense, since his own textual 'sources' have so often done the same thing. Moreover, 'pungent' sauces are specifically an anti-milk: they burn, pierce, separate, while milk creamily soothes and reunites. In this manic orgy Gerontion magically grants himself the oral gratifications that much of the text had assured us were denied. He overcomes the non-reciprocity of the maternal gaze by positing row upon row of mirrors to bolster a Lacanian specular identity. Only 'wilderness' hints at the truly bewildering role the mirror played in 'Portrait of a Lady': 'If the mother's face is unresponsive, then a mirror is something to be looked at but not to be looked into' (*PR*, p. 132). And the constant hint of perverse sexuality and 'Unnatural vices' (*CP*, p. 40) may itself be related to Winnicott's observation that, if the child's experience of mothering proves traumatic, its excessive cathexis of its transitional object will become a source of adult sexual fetishism.

The thwarting contradictions of the subject–object relationship at the centre of 'Gerontion' are far removed from, but not unrelated to, Eliot's evocation of the more benign paradoxes of the relation of art to reality in *On Poetry and Poets* (p. 87): 'it is ultimately the function of art, in imposing a credible order upon external reality, and thereby of eliciting a perception of an order *in* reality, to bring us to a condition of serenity, stillness and reconciliation'. Hillis Miller has suggested that this is Eliot's version of 'an ambiguity basic in romanticism . . . just as Yeats, in *Ideas of Good and Evil*, cannot decide whether the poet "creates" or "reveals" his symbols'.[4] This apparent contradiction between a subjectively imposed order and an objective order that was always already there prompts comparison with D. W. Winnicott's formulation of his central paradox:

the breast is created by the infant over and over again out of the infant's capacity to love or (one can say) out of need. A subjective phenomenon develops in the baby, which we call the

mother's breast. The mother places the actual breast just where
the infant is ready to create, and at the right moment. . . . From
birth, therefore, the human being is concerned with the problem
of the relationship between what is objectively perceived and
what is subjectively conceived of . . . the paradox, as when a
baby creates an object but the object would not have been created
as such if it had not been already there.   (*PR*, p. 13)

Eliot's poetry and drama operate at precisely this interface of subject
and object, whose remote biological root is the initial complexities
and perplexities of the infant–mother relationship; and more often
than not his texts record a failure there, some unimaginably
traumatic breakdown which intensifies aggression towards the
object and which mobilises frenetic defences of manic denial.

Nowhere is this breakdown clearer than in Eliot's doctrine of the
'objective correlative', a concept he could surely only have
formulated while contemplating Hamlet's fraught relationship to
his mother. What is striking in Eliot's discussion of the play is his
eager adoption of the scholarly conclusions of J. M. Robertson.
Pronouncing these to be 'irrefragable', Eliot declares 'that
Shakespeare's *Hamlet*, so far as it is Shakespeare's, is a play dealing
with the effect of a mother's guilt upon her son, and that
Shakespeare was unable to impose this motive successfully upon the
"intractable" material of the old play' (*SE*, p. 143). Making over
Hamlet from Sophoclean to Aeschylean mould, Eliot once again
enacts that effacement of the father which I have so often had cause
to note in the poetry and drama. Hamlet's problem is not to restore
the law of the father by destroying Claudius but simply to cope
with the guilty Gertrude. This, however, he is unable to do:
'Hamlet (the man) is dominated by an emotion which is
inexpressible, because it is in *excess* of the facts as they appear . . .
his disgust is occasioned by his mother, but . . . his mother is not an
adequate equivalent for it; his disgust envelops and exceeds her'
(*SE*, p. 145). This is a mirror version of the strategy of *The Family
Reunion*: Amy was an adequate equivalent for her son's psychotic
state of mind, but the play anxiously assured us that it enveloped
and thoroughly exceeded her, a numinous 'election' not explicable
in this world. Had Eliot read Klein, he might have recast his
account of Hamlet in terms of her psychic positions, to the effect
that Hamlet, fixated in the paranoid–schizoid organisation, has his
most intense relationships with the *internal* objects of his own

phantasy world, and that these relationships have a primitive force out of all proportion to the real objects in the external world to which they are none the less related. Blithely ignoring his own caveat against critics who find 'vicarious existence' in Hamlet, Eliot proceeds to rewrite him as precursor of the psychic dilemma of his own texts.

Failing to attain 'complete adequacy of the external to the emotion', *Hamlet* is a stark reminder of the need for an 'objective correlative': 'a set of objects, a situation, a chain of events which shall be the formula of [the] *particular* emotion; such that when the external facts, which must terminate in sensory experience, are given, the emotion is immediately evoked' (*SE*, p. 145). But this is not altogether the reconciliation it claims to be. Art's earlier cautious 'eliciting' of an objective order in reality is here replaced by a categorical assertiveness – '*shall* be the formula' (emphasis added) – and 'formula' itself implies a remarkable externality of relationship between emotion and its objects. The doctrine of the objective correlative acknowledges an initial division between subject and object, but immediately, in a surge of psychic omnipotence, legislates that gap away, a process that seems fittingly described as a strategy of manic denial. But at the very same time emotion's incarnation of itself in objects and situations does not really affect its initial self-sufficiency. More a Platonic Idea than a Hegelian *Geist*, it is only *contingently* related to its objects, casually alighting on a narrative here or an image there. Magnanimously prepared to embrace them, it does so only in the secret certainty that they are all ultimately disposable. But the Bradleyan Eliot of *Knowledge and Experience* knew that feeling and object mutually defined each other, were integrally and internally bound each to each, not just mechanically hooked together.[5] Ambiguous as everything else in Eliot, the objective-correlative theory dolefully concedes that there is no relation with the object even as it proudly claims that it never needed one in the first place.

The objective correlative is not only the formal goal of Eliot's poetry, but also a frequent thematic concern, and it is characteristically the breakdown between subject and object that is recorded. The fog in 'Prufrock' curls about the house and falls asleep in a tantalising allegory of what a genuine reconciliation of feeling and object might be. In 'Preludes' the poet's fancies are 'curled / Around these images, and cling' (*CP*, p. 24), but the momentary hesitation at the comma, as if they were not quite sure that they were welcome, and then the over-insistence of 'cling', as if they were going to make themselves at home regardless, warns us that unity is more willed than achieved. Between the potency and the existence in *The Hollow Men* 'Falls the Shadow' (*CP*, p. 92). This sombre blankness may be compared with Winnicott's study of a schizoid patient whose deprivations in early childhood have meant that now 'the only real thing is the gap; that is to say, the death or the absence or the amnesia . . . the important communication for me to get was that there could be a blotting out, and that this blank could be the only fact and the only thing that was real' (*PR*, p. 26). And the world ends not with a bang but an infantile 'whimper' as the mother's absence or unresponsiveness conclusively exceeds the text's capacity to cathect the good imago, the solemn eyes of death's other kingdom.

To conclude this study I want to return to *The Family Reunion* and its account of the objective correlative. For here the breakdown is not the result of some inarticulable Shadow, but is explicitly related to the domineering mother. Harry movingly evokes 'the unrecapturable emotion / The glow upon the world, that never found its object' (*FR*, p. 52), and only moments earlier Mary had suggested why this should be so. Discussing their childhood, Harry asks, 'Why were we not happy?' To which comes the reply,

> Well, it all seemed to be *imposed* upon us;
> Even the nice things were laid out ready . . .
> There was never any time to *invent* our own enjoyments.
>   (*FR*, pp. 49–50; emphasis added)

In one sense the tentative forays of subjectivity have encountered a maternal environment so attenuated that they have found no point of purchase; in another they have encountered a world of such impermeability that they have returned mortally bruised from the encounter. There is an absent Mean here which would be a kind of maternal 'slimness' or potential space. In Mary's speech the terms of Eliot's definition of the function of art are reversed: no longer does the subject impose an order on external reality, thereby eliciting an order in reality, but reality instead crushingly imposes an order of its own. In Winnicott's terms, infantile omnipotence has been too soon or too abruptly disillusioned. Maternal neglect, the absence of the object for the 'unrecapturable emotion', has led to too swift a recognition of the breast as a real and autonomous entity; immediate experience crystallises out into a world of resistant surfaces, of hard edges and angles. Neglect thus becomes imposition: where there was once no object there are now a host, each noisily insisting on its depressive independence and rudely brushing aside the subject's cautious salute. Hence the pathologically depressive strain in Eliot's own work, which is a way of being more inhuman, clean and dignified than the objective world itself. But there is a Kleinian side to all this. The 'imposition' Harry has suffered as a child is also an appropriation by the phantasy of the mother: forced to be the phallus for her, he is fixed in the psychotic world of the dual relationship. In a way this too is a neglect, because the mother is relating to the phantasy child of her unconscious more than to the real one squalling in her arms. But the attempt to labour out of this paranoid–schizoid position is rendered extraordinarily difficult because the subject is at the same time seeking a way back *in* to escape the rigours of an existence that is also pathologically depressive. In *The Elder Statesman* a momentary poise is attained. Claverton emerges from a fixated dual relationship with Monica and yet manages to return to energising sources of psychotic phantasy as he faces the two split memories from his past; he does all this *and* manages to be the father whose effacement in the Eliot *oeuvre* had caused all the bother in the first place.

In a famous statement Eliot described the poet's mind as 'constantly amalgamating disparate experience' whereas the ordinary man's experience is chaotic and fragmentary: 'The latter falls in love, or reads Spinoza, and these two experiences have nothing to do with each other, or with the noise of the typewriter or the smell of cooking; in the mind of the poet these experiences are always forming new wholes' (*SE*, p. 287). In the 'smell of cooking' we recognise again the presence of the woman who 'keeps the kitchen' in 'Gerontion' (*CP*, p. 39), and the task of this study of Eliot has been to 'rescue' her from just such marginalisation. Yet at the same time she hardly needs my rescuing. In the context of Eliot's poetic *oeuvre*, 'smell of cooking' will also evoke those more alarming female smells which are ultimately traceable to the slow stewing of woman's heated metabolism, and the poet taps away at his typewriter in a struggle to batten down those terrors. I have tried to illuminate the 'new wholes' that are forged therefrom. Marginalised and ubiquitous at once, the woman is both securely stowed within the kitchen and as unlocatably pervasive as a strong smell.

The fascination of Eliot's poetry is precisely in the fraught *dialectic* of its psychic impulses, which may be defined by contrast with that least satisfying strand in his work that is so heavily dependent on splitting and idealisation. The introductory note to *The Dry Salvages* serves as an instance: 'The Dry Salvages – presumably *les trois sauvages* – is a small group of rocks, with a beacon, off the N.E. coast of Cape Ann, Massachusetts. *Salvages* is pronounced to rhyme with *assuages. Groaner:* a whistling buoy' (*CP*, p. 205). *Les trois sauvages* are at once identifiable as the three dangerous sirens of the *Waste Land* facsimile, but the full menace of their presence is already offset by a 'beacon' that will later become the Virgin Mary. 'Sauvages' then modulates into 'salvages', a verb that suggests a reparative effort among psychic ruins rather than persecutory fear. But in introducing 'assuages' to modify our initial pronunciation of 'Salvages', Eliot would have us believe that the arduous task of restoration is already over; hence a persecuted '*Groaner*' can metamorphose in an instant into a 'whistling b(u)oy'. But these verbal sleights of hand smack more of omnipotent denial than of a truly depressive mourning: 'assuages' is a little too bland too soon, 'whistling' is too determinedly casual. Located both at sea and by the shore, *The Dry Salvages* will edge nearest of the *Quartets* to Eliot's most sexually charged themes, and its preliminary note – a fine Eliotic text in its own right – is thus a laying of ghosts that might threaten the poem proper. But when such psychic evasiveness is writ large it produces only the *longueurs* of *Ash-Wednesday*.

Eliot's verse is both strongest and strangest in its dialectical representation of women. Eliotic woman does not merely cook (or smell), she is no mean hand with a typewriter herself; at her most vividly physical, she is also a text or a producer of texts. No doubt she has many '*cunn*ing passages, *contr*ived corridors' (*CP*, p. 40; emphases added), and even the full force of a Kleinian splitting hardly avails to keep the components of the forbidden obscenity apart. But at the same time 'passages' are simply short texts, and Eliot's line now operates to suggest that 'cunt', 'cunning' and 'contrived' are etymologically affiliated within the range of meanings 'to find, to imagine, to know'; the sexual and the epistemological are thus in the most disquieting proximity. One hesitates to offer Eliot's poetry and drama as a reservoir of Utopian images to contemporary feminism, and yet it may have a modestly salutory value in mediating between a workaday feminism that risks abolishing sexual 'difference' in its quest for legal and economic equalities, and those celebrants of 'difference' who, in rejecting for women the narrow linearity of patriarchal Reason, run the contrary risk of merely reinstating psychosis by another name. On those admittedly rare occasions when she escapes being 'done in', Eliotic woman suggests the need for a *dialectic* of liberation.

Finally, the most telling tribute to the complexity of Eliot's psychic dialectic is its own escape from the straitened rigours of its 'classicist' phase. 'The Death of Saint Narcissus' and 'Mr Apollinax' work out for themselves the critique of Klein that Adrian Stokes was so painfully to elaborate and which I have articulated with the aid of Winnicott's work. Depressive separating out has a pathology of its own, may itself be a manic defence, while, conversely, the paranoid–schizoid position is not merely to be dismissed as regression and madness. Any fully human separating out will simultaneously involve those aspects of the paranoid-schizoid that Winnicott termed the potential space. Eliot's verse articulates these insights, though it can find no sustained resting place within them. At the same time, however, Eliot does not simply dissolve Klein into Winnicott. In rejecting Freud's postulate of a death instinct, in analysing aggression solely as the consequence of frustration, 'object relations' psychoanalysis is an altogether more consoling doctrine than the harsh pessimism of Freud's late works; and in reading Winnicott, one occasionally misses the grittier and more disturbing vision of a Klein. For Klein's evocation of a ferocious sadism towards the maternal body buried deep within the archaeology of the psyche is a sombre reminder of forces *against* liberation so archaic and powerful as to seem, at least in feminism's bad moments, well-nigh insuperable. And Eliot's value too is finally in his power to disturb and provoke, in a violence towards women so startling as to leave the reader constantly troubled. In 'The Metaphysical Poets' Eliot cites the closing lines of King's beautiful 'Exequy' to his dead wife:

> But heark! My Pulse, like a soft Drum
> Beats my approach, tells *Thee* I come;

And slow howere my marches be,
I shall at last sit down by *Thee.*

Then, casually, parenthetically, as if the point were so self-evident as to be barely worth lingering over, Eliot informs us that 'in the last few lines there is that *effect of terror* which is several times attained by one of Bishop King's admirers, Edgar Poe' (*SE*, p. 284; emphasis added). Terror? On whose part? The husband's, the wife's, the common reader's, or on Thomas Stearns Eliot's? Is the remark a brilliant *aperçu* or self-betraying evidence of obsession? When we can answer these questions with certainty, we shall presumably have done with the poetry and drama of T. S. Eliot, which will have shrunk to the neatly packaged dimensions of a case study. It is Eliot's substantial achievement to have interrogated the elegant schemas of the depressive position, and to have compelled his interpreters to adopt a strategy as 'schizoid' as the poems' own.

Notes

Note to the Preface

1. T. S. Eliot, *Murder in the Cathedral* (London: Faber, 1968) pp. 20, 46, 94, 45, 72.

Notes to Chapter One: Theoretical Preliminaries

1. Sigmund Freud, 'Psychoanalytical Notes on an Autobiographical Account of Paranoia (Dementia Paranoides)', in *Case Histories II*, trs. James Strachey, ed. Angela Richards, vol. IX of the Pelican Freud Library (Harmondsworth: Penguin, 1979) pp. 129–223.
2. For a brief account of Jung that makes some useful contrasts with Klein see Anthony Storr, *Jung* (London: Fontana, 1973); and for a fuller critique Edward Glover, *Freud or Jung?* (New York: W. W. Norton, 1950).
3. Cited in Hanna Segal, *Klein*, Fontana Modern Masters (London: Fontana, 1979).
4. The 'pre-genital' and the 'pre-Oedipal' are not synonymous. The former refers to bodily areas, functions and impulses – oral, anal and urethral – while the latter indicates a configuration of relationships to the parents. I use the term 'pre-Oedipal' to refer to the earliest phase in which the father is apprehended as mere adjunct to the mother, not as the Freudian agent of prohibition. See below, p. 17.
5. The best diachronic account is Segal, *Klein*.
6. Cited in Peter Fuller, *Art and Psychoanalysis* (London: Writers and Readers, 1980) p. 112.
7. See Sigmund Freud, *Beyond the Pleasure Principle*, trs. James Strachey (London: Hogarth, 1974) pp. 30–3, 44–50.
8. Melanie Klein, 'Notes on Some Schizoid Mechanisms', in *Envy and Gratitude and Other Works 1946-1963* (London: Hogarth, 1975) pp. 1–24.
9. Cited in J. Laplanche and J.-B. Pontalis, *The Language of Psycho-analysis*, trs. Donald Nicholson-Smith (London: Hogarth, 1973) p. 210.
10. Melanie Klein, *The Psychoanalysis of Children* (London: Hogarth, 1975).
11. Cited in Terry Eagleton, *Walter Benjamin, or Towards a Revolutionary Criticism* (London: New Left Books, 1981) p. 143. See the use of Hegel in R. D. Laing, *The Divided Self: An Existential Study in Sanity and Madness* and *Self and Others* (Harmondsworth: Penguin, 1965 and 1969).
12. Melanie Klein, 'Symbol Formation and its Importance in the Development

147

of the Ego', in *Love, Guilt and Reparation and Other Works 1921-45* (London: Hogarth, 1975) pp. 220–1.

13. The key statement here is Klein's 'A Contribution to the Psycho-genesis of Manic-Depressive States', ibid., pp. 262–89.
14. Klein, 'Mourning and its Relation to Manic-Depressive States', ibid., p. 369.
15. Sigmund Freud, 'Delusion and Dream in Jensen's *Gradiva*', *The Standard Edition of the Complete Psychological Works of Sigmund Freud*, trs. James Strachey, vol. IX (London: Hogarth, 1966) pp. 3–95.
16. Klein, *Love, Guilt and Reparation*, pp. 210–18.
17. Fuller, *Art and Psychoanalysis*, ch. 2.
18. *New Directions in Psycho-analysis*, ed. Melanie Klein, Paula Heimann and R. E. Money-Kyrle (London: Tavistock, 1955).
19. Sigmund Freud, 'Analysis of a Phobia in a Five-Year-Old Boy', in *Case Histories I*, trs. James Strachey, vol. VIII of the Pelican Freud Library (Harmondsworth: Penguin, 1977) pp. 163–305.
20. D. W. Winnicott, *Through Paediatrics to Psycho-Analysis* (London: Hogarth, 1977) p. xxxvii.
21. Cited in Fuller, *Art and Psychoanalysis*, p. 204. For a comparison of Jung and Klein on this point, see Storr, *Jung*, pp. 44–6.
22. For Lacan the 'mirror phase' is a preliminary fixing or 'roughcast' of the ego, which is the very reverse of what Winnicott intends. See Lacan's 'The Mirror Stage as Formative of the Function of the I', in *Écrits: A Selection*, trs. Alan Sheridan (London: Tavistock, 1977) pp. 1–7.
23. For an exposition of this concept, see Laplanche and Pontalis, *The Language of Psycho-Analysis*, p. 210.
24. Ibid., p. 329.

Notes to Chapter Two: Wrestling with the Devil of the Stairs

1. A. D. Moody, *Thomas Stearns Eliot: Poet* (Cambridge University Press, 1979) p. 39.
2. Eagleton, *Walter Benjamin*, p. 145.
3. Sigmund Freud, *Jokes and their Relation to the Unconscious*, trs. James Strachey, vol. VI of the Pelican Freud Library (Harmondsworth: Penguin, 1976) p. 143.
4. Segal, *Klein*, pp. 45–6.
5. See Michèle Montrelay, 'Inquiry into Femininity', *m/f*, no. 1 (1978) 82–101; and *New French Feminisms*, ed. Elaine Marks and Isabelle de Courtivron (Amherst: University of Massachusetts Press, 1980).
6. Harold Bloom, *Poetry and Repression: Revisionism from Blake to Stevens* (New Haven, Conn.: Yale University Press, 1976) p. 95.
7. Another pre-Oedipal version of Eliot's tradition, rather less comfortable than Winnicott's, is that of Terry Eagleton, who has rewritten 'Tradition and the Individual Talent' as 'Hysteria': 'Eliot's tradition is a self-equilibrating organism extended in space and time, eternally replete but constantly absorptive, like a grazing cow or the Hegelian Idea. Perhaps it is most usefully visualised as a large, bulbous amoeba, whose pulsating body inflates

and deflates, changes colours, relations and proportions, as it digests.' See his *Walter Benjamin*, pp. 54–5.

8. Cited in *Modernism 1890-1930*, ed. Malcolm Bradbury and James McFarlane (Harmondsworth: Penguin, 1976) p. 243.
9. Cited in David Holdcroft, 'From the One to the Many: Philosophy 1900–30', in *1900-1930*, ed. Michael Bell (London: Methuen, 1980) p. 127.
10. Lionel Trilling, *The Liberal Imagination* (London: Secker and Warburg, 1955) p. 144.
11. Adapted from 'Francis Herbert Bradley', *SE*, p. 445.
12. Herbert Marcuse, *Eros and Civilisation* (Boston, Mass.: Beacon Press, 1966) pp. 113, 115, 117.
13. Cited in *1900-1930*, ed. Michael Bell, p. 128.
14. Richard Wollheim, 'Eliot and F. H. Bradley: an Account', in *Eliot in Perspective*, ed. Graham Martin (London: Macmillan, 1970) p. 173. There is a valuable reading of Eliot in the light of Bradley in J. Hillis Miller, *Poets of Reality* (Cambridge, Mass.: Belknap Press of Harvard University Press, 1966).
15. M. H. Abrams, *Natural Supernaturalism* (New York: W. W. Norton, 1973).
16. T. S. Eliot, *Knowledge and Experience in the Philosophy of F. H. Bradley* (London: Faber, 1964) p. 202.
17. Wollheim in *Eliot in Perspective*, p. 183. The Eliot quotation is from *Knowledge and Experience*, p. 133.
18. Hugh Kenner, *The Invisible Poet: T. S. Eliot* (London: Methuen, 1965) p. 31.
19. Michael Edwards, *Eliot/Language*, Prospice 4 (Breakish, Scotland: Aquila, 1976) p. 9.
20. Cited in C. K. Stead, *The New Poetic* (London: Hutchinson, 1964) p. 155.
21. Leo Bersani, *Baudelaire and Freud* (Berkeley, Calif.: University of California Press, 1977) p. 6.
22. Cited in Rosemary Jackson, *Fantasy: The Literature of Subversion*, New Accents (London: Methuen, 1981) p. 90.
23. Kenner, *Invisible Poet*, p. 21.
24. Cited in B. C. Southam, *A Student's Guide to the Selected Poems of T. S. Eliot*, 2nd edn (London: Faber, 1974) p. 18.
25. See T. E. Hulme's 'The Sunset', Richard Aldington's 'Sunsets' and, more voyeuristic than violent, his 'Evening' in *IP*, pp. 55, 58.
26. T. S. Eliot, 'Eeldrop and Appleplex', *Little Review*, IV, no. 1 (May 1917) 7–11, and no. 5 (Sep. 1917) pp. 16–19.
27. Frederic Jameson, 'Imaginary and Symbolic in Lacan: Marxism, Psychoanalytic Criticism, and the Problem of the Subject', *Yale French Studies*, LV, no. 6 (1977) 359.
28. Leo Bersani, cited in Jackson, *Fantasy*, p. 87.
29. F. R. Leavis, 'Eliot's Classical Standing', in *Lectures in America* (London: Chatto and Windus, 1969) p. 42.

Notes to Chapter Three: Carving

1. Cited in *EEY*, p. 68.
2. Richard Cork, *Vorticism and Abstract Art in the First Machine Age*, 2 vols (London: Gordon Fraser, 1976).
3. See also *FS*.
4. See Stephen Heath, 'Difference', *Screen*, no. 19 (Autumn 1978) pp. 84–5.
5. Jean-Paul Sartre, *Being and Nothingness: An Essay on Phenomenological Ontology*, trs. Hazel E. Barnes (London: Methuen, 1958), p. 609.
6. Michèle le Doeuf, 'Operative Philosophy: Simone de Beauvoir and Existentialism', *Ideology & Consciousness*, no. 6 (Autumn 1979) p. 51.
7. Frank Kermode, *Romantic Image* (London: Fontana, 1971) p. 135.
8. Cited in *The Modern Tradition: Backgrounds of Modern Literature*, ed. Richard Ellmann and Charles Feidelson (New York: Oxford University Press, 1965) p. 146; and p. 174.
9. Donald Davie, *Ezra Pound: Poet as Sculptor* (London: Routledge & Kegan Paul, 1965) p. 127.
10. Grover Smith, *T. S. Eliot's Poetry and Plays: A Study in Sources and Meaning*, 2nd edn (Chicago University Press, 1974) p. 34.
11. See Southam, *Student's Guide*, p. 88.
12. Bersani, *Baudelaire and Freud*, p. 66.
13. Ibid., p. 70.
14. Robert Browning, *Poetical Works 1833-1864*, ed. Ian Jack (London: Oxford University Press, 1970) pp. 367–9, 3.
15. It has been suggested that Eliot's allowing his wife to make a rather flagrantly adulterous trip to Brighton with Russell represents an Oedipal need to placate a sexually aggressive father figure. See Harry Trosman, 'T. S. Eliot and *The Waste Land*: Psychopathological Antecedents and Transformations', *Archives of General Psychiatry*, no. 30 (May 1974).
16. Cited in Davie, *Ezra Pound*, p. 98.
17. Cited in Kenner, *Invisible Poet*, p. 72.
18. Sartre, *Being and Nothingness*, p. 607.
19. See Freud, *Civilisation and its Discontents*, in *The Standard Edition of the Complete Works of Sigmund Freud*, trs. James Strachey, vol. XXI (London: Hogarth, 1961) ch. 4.
20. For a related literary discussion of these issues to which I am much indebted, see Terry Eagleton, *The Rape of Clarissa* (Oxford: Blackwell, 1982).
21. Moody, *Thomas Stearns Eliot*, p. 64.
22. See Freud, 'On Narcissism: an Introduction', *The Standard Edition of the Complete Works of Sigmund Freud*, trs. James Strachey, vol. XIV (London: Hogarth, 1957) pp. 69–102.
23. Kenner, *Invisible Poet*, p. 198.
24. Cited in Fuller, *Art and Psychoanalysis*, p. 147.

Notes to Chapter Four: Not Waving but Drowning

1. Joseph Conrad, *Heart of Darkness* (Harmondsworth: Penguin, 1973) p. 107.
2. See Adorno's *The Philosophy of Modern Music* (New York: Seabury Press, 1973).

3. Jackson, *Fantasy*, p. 15. See also F. N. Lees, 'Mr Eliot's Sunday Morning *Satura*: Petronius and *The Waste Land*', in *T. S. Eliot: The Man and his Work*, ed. Allen Tate (Harmondsworth: Penguin, 1971) pp. 343–52.
4. John Peter, 'A New Interpretation of *The Waste Land* (1952)', *Essays in Criticism*, no. 19 (1969) p. 143. James Miller, *T. S. Eliot's Personal Waste Land: Exorcism of the Demons* (London: Pennsylvania State University Press, 1977) is a book-length version of the same argument.
5. Kenner, *Invisible Poet*, p. 140.
6. Bernard Bergonzi, *T. S. Eliot*, 2nd edn (London: Macmillan, 1978) p. 95.
7. August Strindberg, *The Father, Miss Julie and The Ghost Sonata*, trs. Michael Meyer (London: Eyre Methuen, 1976) p. 170. Subsequent references are included in the text.
8. Southam, *Student's Guide*, p. 87.
9. Cited in George Steiner, *After Babel: Aspects of Language and Translation* (Oxford University Press, 1975) p. 35.
10. Jacques Lacan, *The Language of the Self: The Function of Language in Psychoanalysis,* trs. Anthony Wilden (New York: Dell, 1968) p. 31.
11. D. W. Harding, 'What the Thunder Said', in *The Waste Land in Different Voices*, ed. A. D. Moody (London: Edward Arnold, 1974) p. 25.
12. Moody, *Thomas Stearns Eliot*, p. 157. He cites Eliot's 'criss-cross' letter on p. 341, n. 33.
13. Graham Martin, 'Language and Belief in T. S. Eliot's Poetry', in *Eliot in Perspective*, ed. Graham Martin (London: Macmillan, 1970) p. 117.
14. Sartre, *Being and Nothingness*, p. 607.
15. D. W. Harding, *Experience into Words* (Harmondsworth: Penguin, 1974) p. 121.
16. Klein, 'Some Reflections on the Oresteia', *Envy and Gratitude*, pp. 275–99.
17. Aeschylus, *Oresteia,* trs. Robert Fagles (Harmondsworth: Penguin, 1977) p. 264.
18. André Green, *The Tragic Effect: The Oedipus Complex in Tragedy,* trs. Alan Sheridan (Cambridge University Press, 1979) pp. 55–6.
19. Green, *The Tragic Effect*, p. 55.
20. Klein, *Love, Guilt and Reparation,* pp. 210–18.
21. Ibid., p. 47.
22. Sigmund Freud, *Beyond the Pleasure Principle*, trs. James Strachey (London: Hogarth, 1974) p. 12.
23. Harding, *Experience into Words*, p. 139.
24. Ibid., p. 145.
25. T. S. Eliot, *The Confidential Clerk: A Play* (London: Faber, 1967) p. 118.
26. T. S. Eliot, *The Elder Statesman* (London: Faber, 1969) p. 32. Subsequent references are included in the text.

Notes to Chapter Five: Stiffening in Conclusion

1. Cited in Kenner, *Invisible Poet*, p. 116.
2. Ibid., pp. 108–10.

3. Roland Barthes, 'Wine and Milk', in *Mythologies*, trs. Annette Lavers (Frogmore, St Albans: Paladin, 1973) p. 60.
4. Hillis Miller, *Poets of Reality*, p. 143.
5. For a fuller discussion see my 'To Criticise the Critic: a Review-Essay', *Literature and History* (Autumn 1982) pp. 248–53.

Index